KICKSTARTER FOR AUTHORS

EMPOWERING WRITERS TO FUND AND FLOURISH

ANTHEA L. SHARP

Fiddlehead Press

CONTENTS

PART TWO
BUILDING YOUR CAMPAIGN, STEP BY STEP

PART THREE
CAMPAIGN STAGES FROM
PRELAUNCH TO FULFILLMENT

PART FOUR
RESOURCES AND NITTY-GRITTY

COMPREHENSIVE CAMPAIGN CHECKLIST

INTRODUCTION

- Why Kickstarter for Authors?
- About the Book
- What Is Kickstarter?
- Advantages of Crowdfunding
- Considerations and Challenges

WHY KICKSTARTER FOR AUTHORS?

I ran my first Kickstarter campaign in March of 2022—the same month that epic fantasy author Brandon Sanderson broke records on the platform by raising $42 million. Forty-two million! That was eye-opening.

Of course, we can't all be Brandon Sanderson, but my first campaign funded a respectable $7,145. I was delighted, and knew that Kickstarter and I were at the beginning of a great partnership. I could see the potential of the platform to help me reach new fans and connect with old ones in a deeper, more satisfying way. As a veteran of both traditional and indie publishing, I was getting tired of launching my books on platforms that mostly wanted to sell ads on my product pages, or signing my rights away to publishers with restrictive, grabby publishing contracts. After fifteen years in the business, the bookselling platforms (and the traditional publishers) had come to feel like frenemies.

Kickstarter felt more like an old friend. I was hooked.

In April 2022, after my *Into the Darkwood* campaign ended so successfully, I was excited about the crowdfunding possibilities. I went on Facebook looking for the communities where authors were talking about the power of Kickstarter...and there weren't any. At least none that were freely open for all authors to join. So I started the Kickstarter for Authors Facebook group. It is (in my humble opinion) one of the best and most supportive communities for authors looking to find out about the Kickstarter platform, as well as a powerful place to connect with other creators for cross-promoting projects.

I owe a debt of gratitude to that group. Alone, I couldn't have developed my knowledge of the Kickstarter platform—and how a wide variety of authors can use it successfully—to the degree I have. Every day I get to see campaigns in all stages: being built, launched, funded, and fulfilled. As a group, the collective wisdom is phenomenal, and I'm so thankful for everyone who's been on the journey with me.

Much of the content of this book first appeared in my posts in the Kickstarter for Authors group. But as new people appeared and asked the same questions over and over, it became clear that organizing and expanding the information into a book would be an excellent idea.

And so, here it is.

ABOUT THE BOOK

Kickstarter for Authors is a comprehensive guide created by a writer (me!), for writers. Drawing on my experiences of running eight successful campaigns to date, plus my deep study of the platform, I'll walk you through every step of crafting a successful Kickstarter campaign, start to finish. From strategizing your project and setting attainable goals to building an enticing campaign page and engaging with backers, we'll leave no stone unturned.

But crowdfunding on Kickstarter isn't just about raising money for your book (though that's a significant perk). It's also about opening up the potential of your writing career. It's about connecting with readers who'll love your work as much as you do. It's about leaving your mark on the world with your words and stories.

It can be immensely dispiriting to feel like you're launching your books into the void, or desperately scrabbling for crumbs on the retailer hamster wheel. I encourage you to step off that path and instead use Kickstarter (and the tools in this book) to begin growing a loyal core of supporters. You'll realize you don't need to price your books in the very bottom of the bargain basement to find readers. You'll also discover the freedom of knowing who your actual readers are, and have the opportunity to meaningfully connect with them.

I've witnessed the power of successful Kickstarter campaigns to help authors get their writing mojo back after intense burnout. I've seen writers get a much-needed confidence boost when a struggling series reached new, appreciative hands, or raised enough funding to defray the costs of publishing. I've also seen authors bring their rabid fans to the

Kickstarter platform and raise $125,000 in the first twenty-four hours. For those authors, Kickstarter offers the opportunity to create special deluxe editions of their books and give other perks to their fanbase that can't be offered on any other platform.

Success on Kickstarter takes many forms: it's not a one-size-fits-all where you must raise thousands of dollars to succeed. There are several intangibles when you create a project that are equally valuable in feeding your creative soul and keeping you energized and engaged. This book will help you figure out how using Kickstarter fits into the bigger picture of your own writing journey.

Whether you're considering launching your very first campaign or wanting to level up your existing tactics, *Kickstarter for Authors* will help you reach your goals. In the upcoming chapters, we'll delve into how to craft a compelling campaign, avoid common pitfalls, set realistic reward tiers, discuss promotion strategies, and much more.

I hope you're excited about joining the hundreds of authors who are using Kickstarter to re-energize their careers and connect with fans in exciting new ways!

*Note: Kickstarter isn't available to creators worldwide. **The platform currently only supports campaigns from creators in AU, CA, most of the EU, MX, NZ, UK, US, Singapore, and Hong Kong.** For authors living outside those localities, check here: When will Kickstarter be available in other countries? – Kickstarter Support

WHAT IS KICKSTARTER?

Kickstarter is a popular crowdfunding platform that allows creators to raise funds for their projects through the support of backers from all over the world. To date, over twenty-two million people have helped fund Kickstarter projects with total pledges amounting to over $7,543,185,142. Most projects on Kickstarter aren't for books, though authors are beginning to turn the Publishing category into an increasingly robust ecosystem.

For you as an author, Kickstarter is a place where you can showcase your book project and find people who'll help you make your project a reality. In return for their financial support, your backers receive your books and any other rewards they pledged to. They become an integral part of the experience as your campaign progresses, commenting and cheering you on as you pass project milestones. There's much more interaction with backers and fans during a Kickstarter campaign than on the usual online book retailers. Kickstarter backers give more, but they also expect more in return.

Unlike some other crowdfunding platforms, Kickstarter isn't a place to raise money for yourself due to hardship, or to beg for financial assistance. The company's mission statement is "bringing creative projects to life," and they do just that. Your job as a creator there is to make a new and compelling project and get backers excited about supporting it. This book will show you how.

Your campaign's main focus needs to be on creating something that's not available anywhere else. That said, your campaigns don't have to be about launching brand-new books. If you have eBooks available but no print versions, you can create a project to bring physical copies into the world. You can offer your eBooks as part of the campaign rewards, but they can't be the main focus of your project.

Additionally, Kickstarter is a Public Benefit Corporation. This means that while they are a for-profit company, they also have a mandate to consider the impact of their decisions on society, not just the needs of their shareholders. They aren't focused solely on profits. They incorporate values like purpose, accountability, and transparency into their business model. It also means that their mission statement comes first. *Bringing creative projects to life* is what the company is all about.

ADVANTAGES OF CROWDFUNDING WITH KICKSTARTER

Still not sure if Kickstarter is for you? Here are some reasons to consider it.

Direct Engagement: Kickstarter allows you to interact directly with your audience, forming deeper connections with readers who are genuinely interested in you and your work.

Raising Money for Your Project: One of the primary reasons to crowdfund is to help defray the costs of getting your book out in the world or pay up front for a more expensive project like an offset print run, a graphic-heavy book, or an audio-book. It's a great feeling to earn back those expenses and launch your books into profit!

Swag and Goodies: Many authors love adding extras to their campaigns. Swag includes things like bookmarks, character art, stickers, and more. And backers appreciate the opportunity to get everything from a nice bookmark to exclusive, goodie-packed book box rewards.

Special Editions: Most high-quality special editions require an offset print run. Unlike Print on Demand, offset printing requires you order a minimum set number of books up front. A Kickstarter campaign can raise the funds you'll need to order those books. Backers effectively "preorder" your books. When your campaign ends, you'll know how many copies to print, have the money to print them, and won't end up with a garage full of books. (At least not for very long.)

Other Formats: Authors are always interested in exploring the audiobook possibilities with Kickstarter. There are important considerations when considering launching a campaign to fund your audiobook (hint: it's not as easy as you think). We'll get into that in future chapters.

Validation: If you've been struggling with low sales or feeling like you're not a legitimate author, a successful campaign— even a small one—can help you see that your books *are* wanted in the world.

CONSIDERATIONS AND CHALLENGES

While Kickstarter offers fantastic opportunities for authors, it's also important to be aware of the potential challenges.

All or Nothing: Kickstarter operates on an "all or nothing" model, which means you must reach your funding goal by the campaign's end to receive any funds at all. Setting a realistic funding goal for your project is essential.

Time and Effort: Running a Kickstarter campaign is a lot of work. It involves planning and preparing your project, engaging with backers throughout the campaign, and delivering on your project promises. Be prepared to invest your time and energy into the process.

Fulfillment Responsibilities: Successfully funded campaigns come with the responsibility of sending out rewards to backers. Be realistic about what you're offering (don't over-promise). Make sure you can get rewards to all your backers efficiently and in a timely manner.

I hope this introduction has answered some of your questions and gotten you excited about the possibilities. The platform has helped many authors find success, and this book is here to help you join their ranks. Ready?

Kickstarter's waiting, and so are your readers.

PART ONE
USING KICKSTARTER LIKE A PRO

CHAPTER 1
GETTING AROUND THE PLATFORM

- Kickstarter Home Page
- Using Search
- The Power of *Discover*
- Publishing Categories
- What to Look for As You Browse
- Become a Backer

Before you start making your own a project, as a creator, it's important to get a feel for how Kickstarter works from the other side, as a backer. The more you understand about the platform, the better you'll be able to use that knowledge to build an irresistible campaign.

It's also important to get familiar with how other authors in your genre are using the platform. Spend some time checking out their projects and seeing what they have to offer.

Let's start from the home page at kickstarter.com.

HOME PAGE

The Kickstarter home page is a busy place. There are tens of thousands of campaigns running at any given time, and it can be overwhelming when you first visit the website. Publishing projects are just a small piece of the pie. How do you find them? Where do you start?

The most important thing to know is that Kickstarter's search is built on a robust "filtering" system. While this makes it a very powerful tool, it can also be very confusing at first glance.

There are two main ways to search the platform, accessible from almost any page on Kickstarter. The first is by clicking the Search and magnifying glass icon on the upper right. The second way is by selecting the word "Discover" on the upper left. Be aware—these two entry points work in different ways.

USING SEARCH

The search tool looks for keywords in all categories. It's great if you know the name of the creator or the title of their Kickstarter project. Typing those in should get you the results you want. But a broader keyword like "dragon" is going to pull up an overwhelming number of campaigns. You'll see everything from comic books to small-batch tea, tabletop games, gaming gear, children's books, and more. Basically, any project that has used the word "dragon" in their title or subtitle will appear.

This is where the filtering comes in. You'll need to narrow down your options via a series of boxes with dropdown menus at the top of the search results page. If you're looking for books, the very first thing you'll want to do is change the "All categories" to "Publishing," and probably narrow that even more to the "Fiction" subcategory. Now you get much more targeted results. However, you still might not be seeing every fiction project with dragons. If the creator didn't specifically put the word "dragon" in their campaign's title or subtitle, it won't be popping up in the search.

Because of this, I generally navigate the sea of campaigns using the Discover option instead of the Search tool. This ensures I'll see *every* project in the Publishing category I'm browsing, regardless of keywords.

THE POWER OF *DISCOVER*

I am on Kickstarter daily to see what's new, to keep an eye on campaigns from folks in the Kickstarter for Authors group, and to gauge the temperature of what's happening with projects in the Publishing category. Here's how I get started browsing.

From the home page (or any page, including my own dashboard), I click "Discover" on the upper left.

This will open up a long menu list. I encourage you to explore those options when you have time, but if you want to keep your browsing streamlined, pick "Just Launched." This will take you to a page with the many-boxes filtering menu at the top. Below are displayed all the most recent campaigns in all categories across Kickstarter. There are way too many to sort through. Time to narrow down those results.

Box 1: *Show me*. Change the first box's dropdown menu from "All Categories" to "Publishing." You can leave this set to "All of Publishing" or limit the results even more by choosing one of the subcategories, like "Fiction" or "Young Adult."

Box 2: *projects on*. I generally leave the location set to "Earth" (alas, other planets aren't an option). You can change this if you're looking for campaigns from creators near you or any other specific locales.

Box 3: *that are*. The "Projects We Love" box is automatically selected. This limits the search results to only campaigns that have been designated as Projects We Love by Kickstarter. I like to glance over the results on this page, taking note of what type of campaigns are being hand-selected by Kickstarter staff for the Projects We Love tag.

Once I'm done checking out those campaigns, I close (X out) the "Projects We Love" box. Now the page results are showing every currently live project in the category I've selected, sorted from most recent to oldest. While this is great information, some of the campaigns are far too new to give me relevant data.

Box 4: *sorted by*. This final box has a lot of interesting options, and I encourage you to look through them at some point. But for the purposes of the current search, I change the selection from "Just launched" to "Ending Soon." This flips the sort order of campaigns from the newest ones to projects that are ending, and thus have been running much longer. This gives a good overview of how these campaigns have fared over the duration of their Kickstarter. You can see what has funded strongly and what's struggling and likely won't succeed. From here, I click directly on the campaigns I'm interested in backing or studying further.

Once I'm done looking at an individual project's campaign page, I return to my filtered results using my browser's back button. If I've fallen down a series of campaign rabbit holes (as happens frequently), I simply re-run the Discover search.

Live campaigns will always be shown first in the search results. If you scroll for long enough, though, you'll encounter some prelaunch projects, then, finally, ended campaigns. Anything pre-2022 probably won't be relevant to your current needs in terms of studying successful projects. Campaigns from even further back provide interesting relics of the past but are not great at projecting what's currently possible.

A Kickstarter campaign, once launched, never disappears off the platform. This includes projects that didn't reach their funding goal, as well as cancelled campaigns. If you're interested in doing some deep dives into historical data, the ocean is waiting.

TAKEAWAY

The best way to navigate around Kickstarter and check out campaigns is via the "Discover" function. Make it your friend! Learn to sort and filter the search results to find exactly what you're looking for. Knowledge is power.

PUBLISHING CATEGORIES

Within Publishing, there are currently seventeen subcategories:

- Academic
- Anthologies
- Art Books
- Calendars
- Children's Books
- Comedy
- Fiction
- Letterpress
- Literary Journals
- Literary Spaces
- Nonfiction
- Periodicals
- Poetry
- Radio & Podcasts
- Translations
- Young Adult
- Zines

Unlike the retailer platforms, a campaign in one category doesn't show up in any other categories, even if it's a good fit. If you're searching for a young adult fantasy anthology, for example, you'll need to check in three different places: Fiction, Young Adult, and Anthologies. You could try typing "young adult fantasy anthology" into the search bar, but depending on how the creator titled and subtitled their campaign, the project might not show up via those keywords.

WHAT TO LOOK FOR AS YOU BROWSE

Now that you know how to navigate the platform, start studying campaigns in the Publishing category. The more you understand how other authors are using Kickstarter, the better prepared you'll be to set up your own successful campaign. Here's what you should be looking for as you explore the platform.

Campaigns knocking it out of the park!

Have you come across an eye-popping funding amount? Click through and see what the campaign is offering. Scroll through the Reward tiers and check out the highest-level rewards. See how many people pledged to the most expensive levels, and try to figure out which tiers are driving the funding. Consider whether the author is bringing a following of their own to the platform. Look at the genre. There are many reasons a campaign can be seeing wild success.

Take a step further back and study how the campaign page is set up. What's the balance of graphic elements to text? Does the author's voice shine through? Is the focus of the campaign clear and enticing? If you see things you'd like to emulate, grab the link and stash it somewhere for later reference.

As mentioned earlier, Kickstarter campaigns don't disappear off the site once they end. You can always go back and reference that project when you're ready to set up your own campaign. Just make sure you're not plagiarizing other creators' content.

Campaigns that don't seem to be funding.

Take note of those projects, too, especially ones that have been live for a while. See if you can figure out why they have little to no support. How do the banners look compared to the projects that are succeeding? How about the title and subtitle? Is the campaign clear about what's on offer? You'll learn as much from the misses as you will the hits.

Campaigns in your genre.

Pay close attention to projects offering something similar to what you think you'll be making. The Kickstarter platform is your best teacher, and it's incredibly valuable in terms of calibrating your funding expectations. Make sure you're drawing the right conclusions when thinking about your own possible projects. Pay attention to whether the campaign is for a deluxe special edition or a regular book, as those are two very different sides of the same coin.

You'll learn a lot by studying the campaign's reward tiers and how they are priced. Beyond that, look at the number of backers for each tier. What are the most enticing rewards? What are the things that aren't garnering much interest from supporters?

Campaigns you want to keep an eye on.

If you come across a project you might want to support at some point, or one you just want to follow but not pledge to, click the "Remind me" button located below the big green "Back this project" button. You'll receive a reminder forty-eight and eight hours before the campaign closes, giving you a chance to revisit it before it ends.

TAKEAWAY

As you browse campaigns, look at what funded, what funded strongly, and what's struggling. Pay close attention to projects in your specific subgenre, and bookmark them for later reference. Check out the banner and title/subtitles (often that tells you all you need to know about a project's success or failure). Notice if you, as a prospective backer, are drawn to take a closer look.

BECOME A BACKER

There is no better way to experience Kickstarter than to become a backer! Supporting other creators' projects is a strongly recommended best practice for the following reasons:

Pledging shows you firsthand Kickstarter works.

You'll learn everything. The first step of choosing a reward tier and hitting the Pledge button. Seeing how add-ons work behind the scenes. Receiving messages from the Kickstarter platform, and from the project creator.

You'll see a few different approaches in how creators communicate with backers, and can decide on what feels best to you. You'll understand what backer updates are and how they are delivered to supporters. You'll see where and how you can comment on projects, and experience firsthand how messages and emails are delivered. Once the campaign ends, you'll get the all-important experience of receiving and filling out the backer survey.

Not to mention that all this experience will help you answer questions from your own backers once you launch your campaign.

Anecdotal evidence suggests that backing other people's campaigns will help you when you launch your own project.

Your activity on Kickstarter gives the algorithms something to work with in terms of showing your campaign to the right backers. (Book supporters, one would hope!) It's a good idea to give the platform's recommendations engine something to work with. Authors who have backed almost no campaigns have reported that they were able to get their own, stalled, projects moving again after they went and pledged to other book projects.

Finally, supporting other campaigns shows that you're a part of the Kickstarter ecosystem.

Don't give the impression that you're simply standing there with your hand out, looking for support. Kickstarter has a strong sense of community, and backers like to see that you're a part of it.

TAKEAWAY

Back at least five campaigns before you launch your project. You'll learn a ton, and go into your own project with a much stronger understanding of how the entire Kickstarter ecosystem functions.

CHAPTER 2
KICKSTARTER MINDSET

- What Kickstarter Is Not
- What Kickstarter Is
- Defining Success
- Money Talk
- Good Campaigns Take Time
- Where Crowdfunding Fits in Your Career

As a creator, it's vital to make a couple shifts in your thinking regarding what Kickstarter is, and is not. Misunderstanding the platform is the number one thing that makes authors fail —or *feel* like they're failing—on Kickstarter. Your assumptions will get you in trouble. This chapter is essential reading to help steer you around those pitfalls. Once you understand Kickstarter's unique approach, you can avoid these potential issues.

WHAT KICKSTARTER IS NOT

A retailer platform.

The most important thing for indie authors to grasp is that Kickstarter isn't designed like a retailer sales platform. It is structured differently, especially on the back end when you're creating your project. I've seen campaigns end at unexpected times or accidentally launch weeks before the creator intended them to, because the author assumed that the dashboard worked similarly to the big retailers.

Unlike retailers, Kickstarter will not collect or remit any taxes for you. That's on each individual creator. Check with your CPA to make sure you understand how to report your crowdfunding income.

Thinking of Kickstarter as a storefront also sets you up for disappointment when you treat a pledge as a sale. The entire campaign period is very fluid. Backers are free to cancel or adjust their pledges until the last minute. For example, you might hit your funding goal, then drop below it again if a backer decides to cancel their pledge. This is essential to understand. A pledge is not a guarantee. That money is not in your pocket until the campaign ends and the backer's credit card is charged.

A campaign isn't static, like a retailer's product page. Keep your momentum going and your backers engaged throughout the campaign by using backer updates, stretch rewards, and continuing to make your project dynamic. Don't forget about your supporters once they've pledged.

A donation center.

As mentioned in the introduction, Kickstarter isn't a place to ask for donations due to life difficulties. You probably know someone who has raised funds online for medical bills or to recover from other personal or collective disasters. But Kickstarter is not like GoFundMe. Its mission is to crowdfund creative projects, not raise money for causes. In fact, it's against Kickstarter's rules to fundraise for charity. Build your campaign around what you're offering to backers, not around your personal needs.

A bargain-basement store.

Kickstarter backers are not browsing for discount books. They are seeking interesting-looking projects in their favored genres, unique reads, and beautiful editions. They want to be part of bringing your fabulous project to life. Backers want to support creators. I've even had some backers pledge to my projects without a reward (there's a button for that). They just wanted to see my project succeed. Other backers have increased the amount of their pledge over and above the tier they're supporting. This wholehearted support is one of the most refreshing things about creating projects on Kickstarter.

Like any platform, however, you still need to motivate people to choose your project. Just keep in mind that discount prices aren't the driving factor. If you're setting your eBook pricing to $1 a book, you are not necessarily going to find more backers by using that strategy. Instead, you're only going to keep yourself from making a profit, and risk having potential supporters wonder what's wrong with your books.

The amount of work that goes into creating and running a successful Kickstarter campaign means you need to value your books. Set reward tiers at prices that will make you a profit, especially as you'll reach a far smaller number of people on Kickstarter than on the retailer platforms. Quality over quantity should be your guide.

To make your project more appealing to supporters, add value in other ways. Deliver the books early (before retail release), add extra perks and bonus content, or give a small, limited-time discount to early backers or for book bundles at higher tiers.

TAKEAWAY

Kickstarter is a crowdfunding platform with a lot of nuance. Approach it with as few preconceived notions as possible. Offer higher-margin rewards that will appeal to backers, remember that pledges aren't set in stone until the campaign ends, and don't assume that Kickstarter functions like the retailer platforms.

WHAT KICKSTARTER IS.

Imagine taking a fundraising platform, a social media site, an online retailer, and a newsletter/Patreon/Substack and stirring them all together into one big, colorful conglomeration. Now we're getting closer to what Kickstarter is. Yes, you use it to raise funding for your books. You also can connect with your current fans as well as new supporters who might love what you're offering. It's an interactive place, not a set-and-forget platform. I think of Kickstarter like an event—a kind of online party. Or a garden that goes through the stages of planting, weeding, and watering, until you reach the final harvest.

A product launch.

You are bringing something new to life with your Kickstarter campaign. This is your chance to spotlight what's special about it! Get your fans and supporters excited about this new, wonderful thing that's coming into the world.

Build prelaunch anticipation for your project by teasing some of what your campaign is going to offer. Show off sneak peeks to your readers and highlight what's coming on your social media.

A popup store.

Running a campaign has a lot of similarities to operating a popup store or managing a sales table at an event. It's an ongoing process of connecting with people who pass by, and engaging with them in ways that will encourage them to support what you're offering.

You want people to pledge for your books, yes, but even before that you want to be visible to prospective new fans. Make it obvious what you've got on your table, and set that table up to look good. Then work on making connections with readers who will love your stories. Treat your supporters to swag and goodies. Be a real person, not a faceless author on a huge retailer platform. Kickstarter backers like to know whom they're supporting.

An online party!

I've seen authors make great use of the "reader party" aspect of Kickstarter by going live on their social media platform of choice when they launch their campaign, or when they end. Or both! Authors have also done book cover reveals on their project prelaunch banners, as well as hosted live video events for backers during their campaign. If this sounds fun to you, absolutely embrace this aspect of Kickstarter.

At the very least, you'll want to celebrate with your backers when you hit certain milestones. Reaching your funding goal, unlocking stretch rewards, and ending successfully are all chances to share the joy of seeing your book project come to life.

While Kickstarter has a strong social media aspect, you don't have to interact *all* the time. It is important, though, to respond to questions and comments, both on your campaign and in private messages. (The exception here is spammers promising to help you find backers—those should immediately be marked as spam and ignored.) It's also essential to use your project updates to keep backers in the loop during and after your campaign, letting them know about new things like unlocked stretch rewards or upgraded items you're offering. Ongoing communication is a key part of running a campaign. Don't get up from your table and leave it unattended for most of the event. Don't let the weeds grow.

Some authors spend a ton of money to go to reader events and hope to make a dozen fans. Kickstarter brings these people to your project page and gives you the tools to connect with them. Use it well.

TAKEAWAY

Kickstarter has a strong social media component as well as being a crowdfunding platform. Prioritize the CROWD part (which will help lead to the FUNDING). It can be useful to imagine your campaign like setting up a table at a busy event with a lot of potential readers walking past your booth. (We'll get into what to put on that table soon!) Go into this new endeavor with a shift in your thinking.

HOW MUCH MONEY CAN YOU MAKE?

Most authors have heard by now that in March 2022 Brandon Sanderson raised a record-breaking $42 million (million!) on Kickstarter for four secret novels. Some people will get starry-eyed at the possibilities. Others will be in the opposite camp, thinking they have no audience, and no one will back their project. The reality is, as always, somewhere in between. According to Kickstarter, most successfully funded projects raise less than $10,000.

The key to making money on Kickstarter isn't by setting a high funding goal. It's by working to make an awesome campaign with good, solid (and definitely a few expensive) reward tiers, and get people excited about what you have to offer.

There are several things to take into consideration when trying to determine how much you might make. What kind of project do you plan to offer? How much of a following do you have? What's your profit margin going to be? You know —business. Figuring out the answers to these questions will help give you a realistic idea of how profitable your campaign might be.

What are you planning to create?

All book campaigns are not created equal. Currently, deluxe special edition projects are burning it up on Kickstarter. These are beautiful book campaigns very often funding into the mid five figures, and sometimes in the six-figure range.

If you are *not* planning to make a special edition, don't go looking at those sparkly, blingy projects and assume you can hit a similar funding raise. It's apples and oranges. A plain hardcover or simple paperback will typically raise far less than these collector's editions. And that's fine! Smaller campaigns can offset your costs and will help you build a new fanbase.

When evaluating any potential project, it's important to consider what else you might have to offer. Often, the high funders have extra things at the top tiers: book boxes, workshops and classes, lots of backlist, special swag packs along with fancy editions, Tuckerizations (naming a character for a backer who has paid for the privilege), etc. Frequently, it's not just the book that's raising the dollars.

If backers are each pledging in the hundreds of dollars for the book box tier delivered over the course of a year (Sanderson), then of course the funding raise is going to be much higher. So is the work involved.

Will your readers follow you to Kickstarter?

One of the great things about Kickstarter is that you don't need a big fanbase to have a successful campaign. This is one of the common misconceptions that authors use to talk themselves out of using the platform. But it's not true.

However, while the Kickstarter algorithms help interested backers find your project page, it's important for you to get the ball rolling. Even if you don't have a large following, you certainly know some people who would support you. Encourage them to do so!

You'll need to spread the word to your readers via social media and your newsletter. There's a section later in this book that lays out some promotional strategies. The good news is that projects in the Publishing category that garner twenty-five or more backers have a stunning 83% success rate. It's not an impossible number to hit, by any means. Every single supporter you bring to the platform helps.

The record-breaking campaigns are ones where authors bring a huge following to the platform. On the flip side, even if you have a large fanbase, you can't dump a poorly-set-up campaign on the platform and expect sudden riches.

Funding amount isn't pure profit.

While some campaigns are pulling in big dollars, there are usually higher costs associated with those projects. These costs include the logistics of fulfilling several hundred (or thousand) book orders.

While it's likely that a campaign that ends up raising $50,000 will have a decent profit, the question remains: what is the *profit margin*? I personally know authors who have run campaigns for beautiful special editions and book boxes that funded over six figures. Those projects barely broke even because there wasn't enough profit margin built into the reward tiers. Those authors lost a couple months of writing time, got some extra gray hairs, and decided that it was *not* worth their time and energy to run another Kickstarter.

I've also seen smaller, less demanding campaigns that raised a thousand dollars but ended up with a 75% profit. These authors walked away with an extra $750 in their pocket, and look forward to running larger, profitable campaigns in the future. It's not how much you make. It's how much you keep.

The ballpark most campaigns are shooting for is 50% profit. After you deduct Kickstarter and credit card fees (around 10% off the top of your final funding raise), pay for making your physical books and swag, and factor in shipping costs, you should try to keep around half of what you raised.

Have realistic expectations.

When planning your first Kickstarter campaign, it's important to have realistic expectations. Remember that Kickstarter reports that most successfully funded projects on the platform raise less than $10,000.

It's essential to look at currently running campaigns in your genre with rewards similar to what you plan to offer. Funding on the platform can vary month by month and genre by genre. The Kickstarter for Authors group regularly has posts from authors breaking down their completed campaigns and discussing the pros and cons of how their project went. You can learn a lot from others.

As of this writing, there's a very good chance you'll be able to raise $500 for a first-time project for a single book, regardless of genre. If you write in fantasy-adjacent genres, double that. You can easily raise more if you're an author with a backlist, a following, and a great-looking campaign. I recently watched a debut book by a new author fund over $15k. It was a gorgeous campaign, but it wasn't for a special edition with any extra bling. It was, however, fantasy, and she did have a previous following on a different platform. As I said above, having some fans and readers makes a difference.

When looking at what you might make from your book project, consider this: most traditional publishing advances for genre fiction have fallen in the sub-$5k range. You could potentially raise that amount, or even more, by creating a project via Kickstarter, without signing away any of your rights. Crowdfunding a project gives authors options. We get to decide what direction to take our careers.

A few campaign examples.

Below are the funding amounts for my campaigns through September 2023. For more in-depth breakdowns of these eight campaigns, see the Campaign Breakdowns and Takeaways section at the end of this book.

Note: None of these were fancy editions and all used Print on Demand printing (mostly from Ingram).

Campaign One: Fantasy hardcover omnibus of a backlist trilogy, March 2022. Funded $7,145 from 133 backers.

Campaign Two: Steampunk paperback collection of short stories, backlist, June 2022. Funded $5,623 from 165 backers.

Campaign Three: Niche art book, August 2022. Funded $2,554 from 74 backers.

Campaign Four: Fantasy/GameLit 10th anniversary hardcover editions, Books 1-3. October 2022. Funded $18,600 from 261 backers.

Campaign Five: Romantic fantasy paperback collection of short stories, new release, February 2023. Funded $7,701 from 228 backers.

Campaign Six: Fantasy/GameLit 10th anniversary hardcover editions, Books 4-6, May 2023. Funded $15,442 from 172 backers.

Campaign Seven: Nonfiction, all formats, new release (this book!), August 2023. Funded $11,251 from 497 backers.

Campaign Eight: Historical Romance paperback, backlist title, September 2023. Funded $1,465 from 70 backers.

In total, I've raised almost $70k via these Kickstarter campaigns. Not all my projects have been huge. As you can see from my most recent campaign, non-fantasy historical romance doesn't have a strong following on the platform (yet). But it doesn't hurt to test the waters with a simple, low-stress campaign. My profit margin on that project was still over 60%.

I have author friends who have raised nearly $200k over the last eighteen months, mostly via special edition hardback campaigns. I have other author friends who have funded far less but are extremely satisfied with the results, including the intangible benefits.

TAKEAWAY

Chances are good you will be able to have a profitable first campaign. For the most realistic idea of what you might be able to raise, search out your genre on Kickstarter and look at the currently running campaigns. Study them closely. They will teach you almost everything you need to know about how your own project might fare.

DON'T FORGET THE INTANGIBLE BENEFITS

A successful Kickstarter campaign can be lucrative, but it's important not to overlook the non-monetary benefits, too. You will get far more from running a Kickstarter campaign than just the funds you raise.

Some authors have found that their campaign helped revitalize a struggling series. Others have gotten their writing mojo back when they discovered readers happy to pay full price for their books. Success doesn't have to come in five figures. I've known authors who've funded "smaller" campaigns and come away completely jazzed about how the project went. Modest success is still success. It's a strong place to build from.

Kickstarter helps authors reach new readers. On my campaigns, frequently over 50% of my project backers come from the Kickstarter platform. These are people new to my work. The number of readers on Kickstarter is only growing as word spreads that the platform is a great place to get books.

I think that even recouping some of the production costs of your book, like editing, graphic design, and covers, is a win. It gives your book a healthy head start. It's a great feeling to go into your retail release with your project already in the black.

Other intangibles include holding that foiled edition hardcover of your dreams, finally getting that audiobook made, and, especially, interacting with fans who are as excited about your project as you are.

Success breeds success. Using Kickstarter will force you to up your marketing game. Making that hooky, trope-filled story intro, describing your characters in irresistible terms, and knowing what makes your book unique and wonderful are all skills you will need to hone for a successful campaign. Once you create those assets, you can use them anywhere else. Making a project on Kickstarter will turn you into a better bookseller everywhere you go.

GOOD CAMPAIGNS TAKE TIME

Expect the entire process of running your first Kickstarter to spread out over a few months. Research, setting up your campaign, prelaunch period, live, and post-campaign fulfillment will all take time.

It's advisable to have your book done, or close to done, when you launch your first project. Running a Kickstarter campaign can be time- and energy-consuming. Many authors report that they thought they'd be able to focus on writing or editing while their campaign was running, but found they didn't get as much done as they'd intended.

A realistic scenario, start to finish, would be three months, assuming your book is done and it's not a special edition being printed overseas.

- 2-4 weeks building your project.
- 2-3 weeks prelaunch period.
- 3-4 weeks campaign is live.
- 2-week wait to get your money from Kickstarter, and send surveys.
- 2-6 week shipping (depending if you have books on hand, etc.).
- 2-4 weeks dealing with straggler issues.

That comes to twelve weeks, minimum, for running a campaign from start to finish. You won't be working on it full-time, but it's important to have a realistic schedule.

Here's a more detailed breakdown of the timeline.

Building your project: This can take up to forty hours (or more), especially if you're spending time researching other campaigns, nailing down your printing and shipping costs, sourcing artwork, etc. *Time: 1 week - 3 months*

Prelaunch: Once you have the basics of your campaign built out, you need to get a prelaunch page up on Kickstarter. General advice is to have that prelaunch page up for two weeks, minimum. Longer is better. I've known authors who've had a prelaunch up for a year. My longest has been about four months.

It's not impossible to have a successful campaign without a prelaunch, but it is definitely harder.

Plan on roughly two to four weeks for prelaunch. The upside is that you can continue to work on and tweak your campaign behind the scenes while your prelaunch page is up and gathering followers. *Time: 1 - 12 months*

Campaign length: Recommended length is seventeen to thirty days. I've seen successful campaigns run as short as ten days and as long as the full sixty allowed. But for your first project, shoot for somewhere in the three-week range. *Time: 3 weeks*

Post-campaign: You'll want to wait at least one week after the end of your campaign before you send surveys or start delivering rewards. Often, creators wait until Kickstarter releases funds to their bank account, which takes about two weeks from your campaign close.

When ready, you'll want to send out your backer surveys to gather information about where to deliver your rewards (both digital and physical). Backers don't always respond right away, so build in a little extra time here, as well. *Time: 3 weeks*

Fulfillment: This depends on whether your book is finished. Hopefully it was done before you launched. Rewards can be sent out as soon as you receive your money from Kickstarter and get the surveys back.

For fulfilling digital rewards, most authors use BookFunnel. Sending links to your backers or bulk-delivering the eBooks is a fairly quick process once your books are set up on BookFunnel.

Print fulfillment will take longer. Even if your living room is already full of boxes of books ready to ship, this part can be time-consuming. How many books can you sign and box up in a day? Once you get them in the mail, plan for two weeks for backers to receive them (for non-international orders).

When ordering your physical books, make sure to factor in the time needed to print and ship. Shipping times get longer around the winter holidays. Hardbacks take longer to print than paperbacks. I've waited up to a month from placing an order to receiving my hardbacks from Ingram US. Drop-shipping from the printer can also run into delays.

If you're planning an offset print run, plan for even more time, especially if you are using an overseas printer. Plan on a minimum of three months, plus another two to three weeks after you get the books to sign and package and ship them out again. *Time: 2 weeks to 4 months+*

TAKEAWAY

Running a Kickstarter can be a lengthy process. Plan for it. When making promises to backers about when rewards will be received, it's always best to under-promise and over-deliver. Be as accurate as possible in your estimates of how much time this is all going to take.

WHERE CROWDFUNDING FITS IN YOUR CAREER

There are dozens of ways to use Kickstarter as an author. There's no one-size-fits-all approach. That's the beauty of it. Personally, I've used Kickstarter to launch new books, bring out anniversary editions, make omnibus hardcovers, put backlist books into paperback and hardcover, and create an art book, and am (finally) setting up a special edition campaign. You can do all, or none, of those things. Just make sure to study the best practices highlighted in this book. They can be applied to a wide range of projects.

At the very least, consider launching your next book on Kickstarter before you release it on the retailer platforms. There's very little cannibalization of sales and you can recoup some, if not all, of your publishing costs. Why not launch your book in the black and start growing your supporter base on Kickstarter?

TAKEAWAY

With Kickstarter, as with most areas of publishing, some people knock it out of the park right away. Most of us, however, build our success over the longer haul. If you approach Kickstarter with a long view, you will be able to use the platform as part of a sustainable long-term career.

GRAINS OF SALT

The advice and suggestions in this book are just that—suggestions. There is absolutely no "one true way" to run a Kickstarter campaign. Every author has different books, different aims, and a different audience. Take your particular needs and situation into account when implementing any of the guidelines set out here. For example, if you have a large readership clamoring for your audiobook, and you know you can reliably get them to support you on Kickstarter, then most of the caveats around running an audiobook campaign won't apply to you.

That said—there are best practices around setting up any project! Watch what is happening on Kickstarter. Notice which publishing campaigns fund strongly. Check out how your genre is doing. Study what seems to be working best for book campaigns in general, and your subgenre in particular.

Kickstarter is your best teacher. All the information to help you succeed is there on the platform, in plain sight. Remember that things change, too. Some items that are popular in certain parts of the Kickstarter ecosystem (like enamel pins) aren't as desirable to backers supporting fiction books. Stay connected with your fellow authors, and know when trends are shifting.

TAKEAWAY

Learn what works for others. Then do what works for you. Kickstarter is a great place for innovation, experimentation, and unique voices.

CHAPTER 3
COMMON FEARS

- Why Am I Doing This, Anyway?
- What if It's too Complicated?
- Will There be Enough Reward for All That Effort?
- Do I Have to Offer Lots of Extra Swag?
- Isn't a Kickstarter Campaign Just Glorified Begging?
- What if My Project Doesn't Fund?
- What if Nobody Shows Up for My Campaign?
- Mistakes: They Can be Fixed
- Can I Lose Money on My Kickstarter?
- Should I be Scared of International Shipping?

If you've run successful campaigns before (or are a confirmed optimist), this chapter is optional reading. But if you feel some anxiety at the thought of running a Kickstarter campaign, you are not alone. Many authors have felt the same when approaching the platform for the first time. I hear these concerns over and over. Can I handle the all the details? Will people want what I have to offer? Will it be worth the time and effort I put into it? If you have questions like these, read on. The path forward is well traveled.

WHY AM I DOING THIS, ANYWAY?

When facing your fears, don't forget about the rewards! Kickstarter offers authors some amazing benefits. And who isn't motivated by amazing benefits? Here are just a few:

You will be able to connect with backers in a personal way. There's nothing nicer than receiving a note of support or encouragement from someone who's excited about your books.

Chances are good you'll recoup your up-front publishing costs, and even make a solid profit on your books.

You can treat your fans and backers to awesome extras and bonus swag. It's fun to create goodies for readers that they can't get elsewhere (just don't go overboard and into the red). Plus, campaign assets like bookmarks, character cards, and stickers can be used elsewhere in your book business.

Kickstarter gives creators amazing data about who is supporting your campaign and how they got to the "Pledge now" button, along with all kinds of other delicious metrics.

You get a chance to get creative and offer something off the beaten path. Lots of people who like the weird and quirky are on Kickstarter!

The platform gives you the perfect opportunity to craft beautiful editions of your books, whether you're simply adding illustrations and custom chapter headers or going all the way with foiled and sprayed-edge special editions.

There's no better place to learn how to up your branding, polish your blurb writing, and present your books to prospective readers. Kickstarter is a crash course in advanced marketing, with a direct feedback loop that tells you what's working.

Audiobook funding can become a reality, as long as you set your campaign up correctly.

You get an incredible opportunity to build a base of superfans who will support every project you create. You'll reach new readers and start building a fanbase on Kickstarter who loves what you're offering. I promise.

WHAT IF IT'S TOO COMPLICATED?

Kickstarter, like any platform, has a learning curve. But luckily for you, there has never been a better time to learn how to create a successful book campaign on Kickstarter. On any given day there are dozens of beautiful book projects up and running on the platform for you to learn from. There is the Kickstarter for Authors group on Facebook, where generous and experienced authors discuss campaigns and share what they've learned. There are books like this one to distill all the wisdom and best practices into one handy reference. There are free classes, and panels from the 20Books Conference about Kickstarter freely available on YouTube. (Please check out the Resources section at the back of this book for more information.)

True, no one is going to spoon-feed you success. Getting your first project set up takes initiative and perseverance and common sense. But you're an author. You can invent entire worlds, craft them into sentences and paragraphs, and package them attractively for sale. You've got skills. You can definitely learn how to run a Kickstarter campaign if you so desire.

WILL THERE BE ENOUGH REWARD FOR ALL THE EFFORT I PUT IN?

Ultimately that's a question only you will be able to answer. Successful Kickstarter campaigns can be modestly to massively profitable (though the massively profitable campaigns tend to happen for authors with large and devoted fanbases excited to get the author's book and extra goodies as soon as possible). If you are one of those authors, Kickstarter is very likely to be rewarding and worth the effort. On the other end of the spectrum, if covering the production costs of your book project and profiting a few hundred to a few thousand dollars on a book campaign sounds like enough reward for you, such results are achieved frequently on first-time campaigns.

A successful Kickstarter campaign will give your book a healthy head start in life, too. Even more importantly, you'll acquire valuable skills that will make your next Kickstarter project easier and more profitable. After all, learning how to use a platform that is working well for other authors is definitely an upside. Once you get past your fear, maybe you'll discover that Kickstarter is for you. I encourage you to try, and not let worry stop you from doing something that could be amazing for your career.

What if you love it? Many authors discover they really enjoy running Kickstarter campaigns. The experience is creative, exciting, and satisfyingly interactive. If it turns out that you are one of those people, then the campaign experience itself will be part of the reward. You may well find it to be the funnest way you ever sold a book.

Remember the intangibles. It's great to connect with backers who really want to support you—even if it's just a handful of folks. It's fun to make swag that you can also use for reader goodies, signings, etc. long after the campaign is over. Don't forget the opportunity to commission or get new artwork and covers. And nothing forces you to up your marketing game better than learning how to set up an enticing campaign. Then you can take those lessons back to your retailer product descriptions and blurbs. For me, the opportunity to get off the retailer hamster wheel, have more control over my books, and directly reach readers has been invaluable and incredibly freeing. I hope it will be for you, too.

DO I HAVE TO OFFER ALL SORTS OF EXTRA SWAG BESIDES MY BOOKS?

Good news! You can have a successful Kickstarter campaign *without* offering any over-the-top extras. While some authors lean hard into all the goodies and add-ons, you don't have to.

Things like signed books, hardcovers, fancy formatting, character art, book boxes, etc. are all optional. You can certainly go that way, and those are often elements of a higher-funding campaign. But it's also important to be aware of how these extras might impact your bottom line in terms of your profit margin.

I have run super-simple campaigns that offered the book in all formats plus a few digital goodies related to the campaign (a Top Tips Hotsheet for the Kickstarter for Authors campaign, a gingerbread recipe for *The Duke's Christmas*).

It's easy to look at some of those swag-ful projects and despair—but take heart. If swag and merch is not your thing, you are under no obligation to offer it. There are other ways to make your project special.

ISN'T A KICKSTARTER CAMPAIGN JUST GLORIFIED BEGGING?

Sometimes, people feel embarrassed about using Kickstarter to help fund a project. *Isn't it like one of those sites where people tell their sad stories and ask for people to help them out?*

Actually, no. It is not. In return for their pledge of support, a Kickstarter backer gets something they want, which is usually your book. Explain to your readers that the platform is another way to preorder books and to help get formats made —like special editions—that wouldn't otherwise be possible. Let your fans know that their direct support means the big companies aren't taking a big bite out of your royalties. You also get the flexibility of delivering all kinds of extra rewards that just aren't possible when someone buys your book off a retailer platform.

Because the funding is all or nothing, there's no risk for people when they support your project. Their credit cards aren't charged until the campaign is over, and not charged at all if your project doesn't fund successfully.

Reassure your friends, family, and readers about the true nature of Kickstarter, and explain why you're planning on using it to help create your next book project.

WHAT IF MY PROJECT DOESN'T FUND?

Even though it might feel terrible, it's not the end of the world. In fact, around 60% of Kickstarter campaigns fail. But according to Oriana Leckert, head of Kickstarter's Publishing category, 82% of Publishing campaigns with at least twenty-five backers succeed!

Sometimes things happen, though. Platform glitches, unexpected life upheavals, etc. can derail your campaign. The good news is that there's no penalty for running an unsuccessfully funded campaign (except in your own mind, of course). I recently saw an epic fantasy author whose first two campaigns failed to reach their goal. He persevered, and his most recent campaign (third one to fund, fifth one on the platform) ended up raising over $30k.

In my opinion, the only real failure on Kickstarter is never launching your campaign. Those projects fail to fund 100% of the time.

WHAT IF I MAKE A CAMPAIGN AND NOBODY COMES?

The worry that no one is going to support your campaign is one of the most common fears I hear from authors considering using Kickstarter. It's easy enough to imagine (we're authors—we're good at imagining the worst). The main character announces a party. The invitations are sent, the table set, the music plays…and no one shows up.

But Kickstarter *wants* to connect you with backers who'll love what you have to offer. Provided your campaign is well crafted, you could get up to 80% of your backers directly from the Kickstarter ecosystem. That said, most creators see at least a small percentage of new supporters come their way via Kickstarter, and up to 50% isn't uncommon.

You absolutely should bring your own fans and supporters to the table, but do some of that work up front, and Kickstarter will help you along. Continue to spread the word throughout the duration of your campaign. Creator cross-promotion can help move the needle, as well as regular posting on social media and keeping your newsletter subscribers in the loop.

Don't have a mailing list yet? Time to start one! Check the Resources at the end of this book.

WHAT IF I MESS UP BIGTIME?

Other than obtaining funding for a project that you never actually deliver (the last book in *Game of Thrones*, perhaps?), nothing will permanently damage your standing on Kickstarter or with your backers. Sure, we all make a few mistakes here and there, but they are recoverable.

I've seen creators accidentally launch their campaigns when they meant to set up a prelaunch page. They powered through (despite not quite being ready) and funded well over their goal.

I've messed up my launch start and end times by not triple-checking my campaign details before I hit the button to go live. That's only one of the many missteps I've made, in fact.

Kickstarter supporters realize we're human beings and independent creators, trying to do the best we can. Clear, open communication goes a long way to help keep our backers on our side and fix any inadvertent mistakes we make along the way.

CAN I LOSE MONEY BY RUNNING A KICKSTARTER?

Yes, if you are careless about your campaign. It's essential to calculate the costs of producing and delivering your book project before you launch your Kickstarter campaign. This is an essential part of setting up your successful project. Fortunately, this book will help steer you around some of the biggest pitfalls. Keep reading.

SHOULD I BE SCARED OF INTERNATIONAL SHIPPING?

Shipping your books overseas can seem daunting at first. I get it! I didn't offer international shipping until my second campaign, once I got a handle on how a Kickstarter campaign even worked. But I've figured it out since then, and you get to benefit from my learning curve. There are some great shipping solutions out there, and some smart workarounds, like drop-shipping POD books from a printing facility and then sending signed bookplates separately. All of this is covered in depth in the later sections on shipping.

TAKEAWAY

Kickstarter campaigns take effort and have a learning curve, but you are not alone. There are plenty of great resources available to help you master a platform that really works for authors. If you're looking for a support network to help you through the process, I highly recommend you come join the Kickstarter for Authors group on Facebook! Kickstarter for Authors | Facebook.

Remember, the only campaign that fails 100% of the time is the one you never launch.

CHAPTER 4
PICK A WINNING PROJECT TO CREATE

- Kickstarter's Rules
- What Will You Make?
- Genre Matters
- What Format Should It Be?
- What About Audiobooks?
- Budgeting Your Campaign
- Figuring Out Printing Costs
- Figuring Out Shipping Costs
- International Shipping
- Hidden Costs
- Where You Can Lose Money
- Adding It Up for a Profit

It's time! You're excited to run a Kickstarter campaign and bring your project to life. But what should that project be? It depends on what you currently have to offer. Will it be a brand-new book, or a backlist project? Your genre might make a difference regarding what you choose to create. The formats you plan to make—eBook, audio, hardcover, special edition—can have a big impact, too.

It's important to get a sense of your budgeting and ROI before you begin, to ensure that your project has the best chance of success and that you don't lose money. There are a lot of moving parts. Take them one at a time. It's all doable.

KICKSTARTER'S RULES

Before you begin, make sure you know what's not allowed on the Kickstarter platform. They have five rules. Familiarize yourself with them at Our Rules — Kickstarter

- Projects must create something to share with others.
- Projects and backer statistics must be honest and clearly presented.
- Projects can't fundraise for charity.
- Projects can't offer equity.
- Projects can't involve prohibited items. Kickstarter will not approve projects that are illegal, heavily regulated, or potentially dangerous for backers, as well as rewards that the creator did not make. Find a complete list at Prohibited Items — Kickstarter

Kickstarter looks at every prospective project on the platform before approving it for launch. Make sure you're staying within their guidelines. For most authors, that shouldn't be a problem.

WHAT WILL YOU MAKE?

Remember that the main point of your campaign must be to make something **new**. The primary thing you're raising funding to create can't already exist in the world.

Fortunately for authors, creating new formats of existing work counts. Bringing out your backlist in paperback and hardcover (if they are not yet in those formats) are excellent choices—especially as Kickstarter backers love physical rewards.

Even when creating something new, that doesn't mean you can't offer your backlist or other formats in your campaign. If you are making a hardcover omnibus of an existing series that's currently available in eBook and paperback, you can still offer those formats as campaign rewards. They just can't be the focus of your project.

Backlist can help any campaign be more profitable. The more books you have to offer backers, the more tiers you can create at higher pledge levels. If you're an author with a backlist, you'll be able to use those books to good effect in your Kickstarter campaigns.

Ready to brainstorm? Here are some projects authors have successfully created for their first campaigns:

- **Brand-new release** in eBook, paperback, hardcover, and sometimes audio (see the audio section for more in-depth look at the challenges of creating an audiobook campaign).
- **Subsequent book** in a series, in the above-mentioned formats.

- **Omnibus or special collector's editions,** often with bonus content.
- **Anniversary editions.**
- **Short story collections.**
- **EBook-only** campaign (a smaller funding goal is recommended if you do this). Digital-only is possible, but many book backers really like their physical copies, so keep your expectations modest and set your campaign up well. That said, digital-only campaigns have a higher profit margin and are easier to fulfill. They just generally don't raise large funding amounts.
- **Print-only** campaign. Several Kindle Select authors have run strong campaigns without providing eBooks, though sometimes they make a digital swag tier available.

Keep things simple by putting a backlist book into a new format.

If you have a lot of trepidation around Kickstarter, I recommend you start with something simple. Put an existing eBook into paperback or hardcover (if you don't yet have one or both of those print formats). Kickstarter backers love physical books, and in most instances the hardcover will be the biggest draw. There are currently a few genres where backers seem to prefer paperbacks, namely cozy mystery, science fiction (somewhat), and contemporary romance. Of course, there are always exceptions. Do your research and let your genre be your guide.

Standalone book.

A campaign focused on a single book can be a nicely contained project. The disadvantages are that you might not have much to add to create higher-cost tiers, so the campaign could end up with a relatively low funding amount. You can increase your average pledge amount by making your book a bit more special. (More on that below.) If you do have a backlist, you can add those books to your campaign. Even if your other books aren't directly connected to your main offering, Kickstarter backers are surprisingly omnivorous. If they like the look of one of your books, they will often scoop them all up.

First in series.

Another approach that has worked for many authors is bringing out paperback or hardcover editions in a series one at a time. If your series is still being written, you will eventually catch up to your newest book, and be able to launch it new on Kickstarter. With this approach, you can see a good build on the platform as you create each edition and make it available to Kickstarter backers first. Ideally, backers will follow you into each new campaign, You should also pick up new supporters along the way. You'll want to offer the other books in the series in digital format as part of this strategy, plus other backlist you might have.

Part of (or an entire) series.

If you've got a smaller series that's complete, like a duet or trilogy, consider running a campaign for the complete set. Or, if you're feeling ready to tackle a bigger project, do a campaign for several (or all) of the books in your longer series. This has the advantage of giving you lots of rewards to offer in one campaign and the opportunity to reach a higher funding amount. The disadvantage is that there are a lot of details involved in creating multiple new editions simultaneously.

Omnibus.

Take a duet or trilogy and create an omnibus collection (all the books under one binding). This can be an excellent strategy, especially if you already have the other print formats available as standalone books. In fantasy, in particular, deluxe special edition omnibus projects are currently all the rage. And speaking of those...

How special *is* a special edition?

As the book ecosystem on Kickstarter continues to grow, more authors are creating campaigns for *deluxe* special editions of their books. Faux-leather covers with foiled designs, fancy page edges that are gilded or colored or feature unique designs, ribbon bookmarks, color interior illustrations —all the upgrades you can dream of, and more. I've seen a gilt-edged fairytale retelling bound in white leather with inset gemstones, and an Oscar Wilde reissue printed on high-end black paper with white type.

But there are varying degrees of special. Some of the upgrades authors can make to books are available via Print on Demand: color interiors, for example, or a case design printed on the hardcover book that's different from the dust-jacket design. Duplex covers (where color images are printed on both sides of the heavy cardstock used for paperback covers) are a nice upgrade for paperbacks. Many authors have figured out how to DIY sprayed edges, too, or hire artists to do so.

You can make your book special by adding Kickstarter-only elements—things that will only be available to backers of your campaign. Exclusive bonus content, illustrations, or a unique cover are always a draw. Other upgrades include signing, personalizing, and numbering each copy on a unique-to-Kickstarter special page that won't be in retailer editions.

Backers will pay more for special editions. The fancier the book, the more you can ask. It is important, however, to make sure you understand the difference between a nicer, upgraded POD and a truly deluxe edition. (I go into more detail about the differences a bit later in this chapter.) When looking at other campaigns to figure out your pricing, make sure you're comparing apples to apples, and not to pearls. Kickstarter backers are supportive but savvy. They are aware when you're overinflating the value of your book.

Launch a new book on Kickstarter.

Got something new ready to go? Before it releases on the retailers, consider launching it on Kickstarter first. Running a campaign gives you the opportunity to cover some, or all, of your sunk costs (things like editing and covers). Why not release your title into the wider marketplace with your book already in the black? Just make sure your backers receive the book at least a month before the retail release date. Three to six months in advance might be even better.

Dream bigger.

Once you get comfortable using the platform, you'll see there's a wide range of options. Or you could just go big with your very first project—it's your choice. How about some of these?

- Fully illustrated editions—black and white or in color.
- Art books.
- Fancy book boxes.
- Oracle or tarot cards to accompany your campaign.
- Letterpress poetry chapbooks.
- Special edition flip books (tete-beche).
- Begemmed editions of fairytale retellings (if you really want to go over the top).

If you can dream it up and pitch it successfully to backers, the sky's the limit. For a first-time campaign, however, it's fine to keep it simple.

Keep in mind that your campaign will ideally draw in backers across three different ranges of interest. You'll be bringing your existing readers to the platform. Some of these readers might only have one or two of your books. Some of them will be your superfans, who already have everything you've ever published. And the last group will be people new to you and your books. Think about each of these groups when you're considering what your project should be, and make sure you provide something that's of interest for all of them.

GENRE MATTERS

The strongest fiction genre on Kickstarter is epic fantasy, beyond a doubt. Spicy paranormal romance also generally does well. Most things fantasy/paranormal/horror adjacent (Epic/Romantic/Paranormal/Horror/Alt   History/Steampunk and, to some extent, Urban Fantasy and GameLit) receive strong support from Kickstarter backers. Fantasy romance finds a warm reception, especially in blingy special editions. Horror anthologies generally have good traction. A well-crafted witchy campaign can see plenty of backers lining up to pledge. Whatever you do, though, spend a little time studying the successful campaigns in your genre to see what other creators are making.

Off-the-beaten-path books often succeed on Kickstarter where they struggle on retailers. The Kickstarter audience likes the quirky and the weird, the nerdy and the fun, the spicy and the silly. If your books are genre mashups or don't fit the mainstream, that's good news! They have a strong chance of finding their readers on Kickstarter. Lean into those aspects as you build your campaign. What makes your books unique and interesting?

Other genres are gaining traction, but in general they will not fund into the multiple five figures (or more) the way the fantasy-adjacent genres sometimes do. Mystery, science fiction (oddly—one would think it would be up with the heavier hitters), and contemporary and historical romance are all genres that are slowly building up supporters and beginning to find an audience on Kickstarter. The exceptions (and there are always exceptions) are those authors, regardless of genre, who have big followings they bring to the platform to help support their project. A strong fanbase will turbocharge any type of campaign.

That doesn't mean you have to write in one of the go-to genres to succeed. I've seen nonfiction do really well, cookbooks, art books, memoir, poetry, children's books, middle grade, anthologies of all sorts. Practically every genre has backers excited to lend their support.

If you're not sure that what you write will find support on the platform, go to Kickstarter and do a search (upper right-hand corner) by typing in your genre and/or subgenre. Try to discover where you stand. Projects never disappear off the platform, so if someone ran a campaign in the past that featured a book similar to what you write, diligent searching should be able to uncover it.

Keep in mind that if a project didn't reach its funding goal, it might not necessarily be because of the genre. It could be because the campaign just wasn't enticing to backers or wasn't set up according to best practices. When looking at older projects, remember that the publishing ecosystem on Kickstarter has shifted considerably for the better since the end of 2021. Recent campaigns are the best predictor of how your campaign might do.

TAKEAWAY

Fantasy-adjacent genres generally have the strongest support on Kickstarter. If you're a multi-genre author, I highly recommend you plan your first campaign around the most fantasy-like books in your catalogue. Quirky, not-quite-to-market books are often appealing to Kickstarter backers, too. Lean into what makes your books unique!

WHAT FORMAT WILL YOUR PROJECT BE?

A deluxe special edition? An audiobook? A regular paperback? An impressively weighty omnibus?

Keep in mind that Kickstarter backers tend to prefer physical rewards. Formats are generally valued as follows, from most desirable to least.

- Hardcover
- Paperback
- eBook
- Audiobook

It's ironic that the thing authors might want the most (an audiobook) is the thing that Kickstarter backers are least interested in.

In certain genres—mostly fantasy—deluxe special edition hardcovers are the most popular type of campaign. In others, like science fiction or cozy mystery, paperbacks are currently supported as much as, or more so, than hardcovers. Genre plays a part. In no genre, however, are digital rewards considered "better" than physical ones.

EBOOK ONLY

It's possible to run a successful eBook-only campaign, as long as you keep your expectations in check. Currently, backers seldom pledge more than $10 for an eBook unless it's an omnibus edition or packed with special options. A $5 tier price is much more common. If you want to raise $1,000, you would need two hundred backers at that level. Keep in mind, most first-time book campaigns from relatively unknown authors see fewer than fifty backers. If you were offering a hardcover at $40, you would only need twenty-five backers to reach that $1,000. It's essential to be realistic about your funding goal and the number of backers you will have.

The authors who regularly do well with all-digital campaigns are typically those who have a well-established following.

Still, there are good reasons to consider a digital-only campaign. EBooks have fewer production details to figure out, no shipping costs, and the entire process tends to be less stressful. The profit margin on eBooks is much higher than on print, and the fulfillment is drastically simplified (most authors deliver via BookFunnel). Just understand that your overall funding amount is likely to be lower than on a campaign with higher-priced physical tiers.

PRINT ON DEMAND VS. OFFSET PRINT RUN

When making a physical book, it's important to know whether you are going to do a Print on Demand (POD) book project, or a paid-up-front offset print run. Some genres, like children's books or art books, are usually created by ordering a print run as opposed to printing one at a time (POD). The advantages of a print run in these cases (and in most cases) is that the cost per book is cheaper. For bigger trim sizes with lots of high-color printing, the savings can be considerable. The downside is that you'll need to order and pay for at minimum fifty copies, and in some cases at least three hundred books, depending on which printer you choose.

If you know your fans will flock to Kickstarter to support your campaign, then consider an offset print run. It's also currently the only way to add high-end special features to your book—things like foil printing, endpapers, ribbon book-marks, digitally illustrated edges, etc. The POD printers don't offer these special features (yet).

By contrast, Print on Demand is super-scalable. You can plan each reward tier so that you cover the costs of production and shipping, plus make a profit. It takes the guesswork out of how many books to order (however many you have pledges for!) and you don't have to commit up front to a minimum number of books. It doesn't matter if you end up with pledges for five books, fifty, or five hundred. Whether or not your campaign takes off, you will be able to fulfill your rewards and make a profit on each one.

Special Editions versus Deluxe Editions

If you're dreaming of something on the fancier side, but committing to an offset print run seems too risky, consider upgrading your POD edition with some nicer features. Here are things you can do with Print on Demand that will make your book a bit more special.

- Interior illustrations / maps / character art
- Gorgeous formatting with two-page chapter spreads
- Under-jacket case designs that are different from the dustcover image
- Color illustrations (especially if you use Bookvault)
- Custom chapter headers
- DIY sprayed edges
- Limited or exclusive version

You can also include things on the author side that add value. Kickstarter backers' names in a special thank-you section. Signed and numbered editions exclusive to Kickstarter. Bonus content only available in the Kickstarter edition. These extras can increase the value of your book. All of these things can also be used as stretch rewards in your campaign. (More on stretch rewards later...)

Keep in mind that the above elements still don't make your book a deluxe edition. Backers expect deluxe editions to include foiled design elements on the dust jacket / case, fancy edges, reversible dust jackets, hubbed spines, ribbon book-marks bound into the book, etc. Make sure you're not misrep-resenting your book project to prospective backers. Don't set your expectations, funding goals, and reward tiers at a deluxe collector's edition level unless you are indeed offering a true deluxe edition, not just an upgraded POD.

A final note: Some nimble authors have pivoted their POD edition to an offset print run mid-campaign when their project took off. The hardcover orders reached the minimum level for an offset print run (usually one hundred books or more). This opened the door for those deluxe features at a similar cost to printing POD. If you find yourself with enough hardcover backers to meet the minimum numbers for an offset print run (100+), it's a good idea to calculate the costs on both options and choose accordingly.

TAKEAWAY

Be clear about the differences between publishing with Print on Demand versus doing a fancy offset print run. For authors with smaller followings (who aren't doing an art or children's book), I recommend you start with POD. You can find a list of printers in the Resources section.

WHAT ABOUT AUDIO?

Many authors look at Kickstarter and immediately think that the platform would be a great way to raise funding for an audiobook. It is—with one big caveat. Almost all successful audiobook projects raise their funding *primarily* on the print tiers.

Audio-only is a tough sell. Why? Kickstarter backers prefer physical books, then eBooks, and, lastly, audio.

One common mistake authors make is thinking of audio as a premium product, since it costs us so much to create. As a result, creators price audiobook tiers way too high. Although some audiobook platforms list retail prices at $25, that's not what most audiobook listeners pay. Listeners use a subscription credit of $12, or Whisper-sync the eBook on Amazon for only $7.50 above the eBook price. Savvy audiobook listeners know how to wait for Chirp sales and use their local library. Virtually nobody pays $25 for an audiobook. They certainly don't on Kickstarter. Exceptions are a huge omnibus, or an audiobook from a big-name author. Cory Doctorow, who has been running very successful audiobook campaigns on Kickstarter for a few years, has slowly been raising his asking price for audiobooks. He's up to $25 now, but his previous campaigns were at $20, and his very first had the audiobook for $15. He grew his audience for audio, and saw good success with that approach.

If you want your audiobook campaign to succeed, set the audiobook tier at an appealing $10-$15. Bundle it with your other formats for an included discount. Most importantly, build your campaign to fund on the print versions of your book, not the audio.

Audiobook campaigns also can fail when the funding goal is set too high. If the audiobook won't get made unless you receive the funding, that makes complete sense. But if you're going to make an audio edition of your book anyway, don't make it an all-or-nothing proposition. Set your funding goal lower and give yourself a chance to defray at least some of the costs by creating a campaign that will fund.

As always, I encourage you to go to Kickstarter and do a search for "audio" or "audiobooks" to see what's currently on the platform. Once you find some projects, it's essential that you dig deeper to understand how the audio is being funded. When you look at these campaigns, *take careful note of what tiers are being supported by the majority of backers.* Each reward tier displays the number of backers for that tier. Use that to guide your own understanding of what backers are pledging for and what tiers are actually driving the funding.

TAKEAWAY

Audio books are, as of this writing, still a tough sell as a standalone on Kickstarter. Your best plan for success is to create a campaign that's about your **book**, in all formats, with audio as just one of the offerings.

BUDGETING YOUR CAMPAIGN

If you want your project to end up in the black, it's essential you do some simple math. Nobody wants to lose money on their campaign, after all! To avoid doing so, there are four key costs to calculate when creating a book project on Kickstarter.

The first is the cost to print physical copies and make any swag you plan to include in your campaign. The second is shipping expenses. The third is the platform and credit card fees that come off the top of your funding raise. The final cost to consider is the core expense of creating your book. This includes things like artwork, editing, etc.

The first three expense categories are generally *specific* to your Kickstarter project. You will need to cover those as part of your campaign, with profit left over for you. You obviously don't want to end up with a project that funds "successfully" but didn't bring in enough to cover the costs of fulfilling your rewards, including making the physical goods, shipping, and fees. This can happen if a creator sets the reward tiers or funding goal incorrectly. If your campaign funds, you are obligated to deliver the promised rewards to backers even if doing so costs you money out of pocket.

The last expense is different. It includes the costs involved in bringing your book to market. Editing, covers, artwork, copy edits—all these are part of running your publishing business. It's important to cover these costs, but in most cases your Kickstarter doesn't need to pay for them. If you're planning to continue selling your book after the end of your campaign, I don't recommend you roll these costs into your funding goal. The profits you make from your campaign can help defray them, but it's generally the job of your retail sales to put you in the black.

The exceptions are projects that either won't go into retail distribution, like a Kickstarter-exclusive collector's edition, or a project that simply can't be made unless you cover the costs via your funding goal. Art-heavy projects and audiobooks have a higher up-front expense. In these cases, it's important to set your funding goal high enough to cover those costs.

FIGURING OUT PRINTING COSTS

Whether you are creating your book via POD or offset printing, you need to know your per-book cost. This is the foundation from which you'll build your reward tier pricing, ensuring you can turn a profit on your campaign.

For a Print on Demand project, you'll need to know your page count, paper color (white or cream), trim size, and type of book (hardcover or paperback). The most popular POD printers—Ingram, Bookvault, Lulu, and KDP—all have online pricing calculators. Use them. Plug in your details and you will get a basic quote for how much a single book will cost to print. With Ingram, make sure you're not looking at the number where they include shipping. At this point, you only want to know the base cost of getting your book printed, which may include tax.

For an offset print run, you'll need to contact a printer (or several) to get a quote. Again, be prepared with your book specs. Find out what the printer's minimum order is. There are only a few printers that have a minimum order of fifty copies. Most of them won't print an order for less than one hundred books, and several require three hundred to five hundred books, minimum. Fortunately, the order amount can often be spread across several titles. A trilogy project could print one hundred copies of each title, resulting in a three hundred total book order. Remember, with offset printing, the more books you order, the lower the per-book cost.

I treat the cost to ship boxes of books from the printer to me as part of the cost of printing the books. I divide the mailing expense by the number of books and include that in the overall per-book cost.

FIGURING OUT SHIPPING COSTS

Shipping is the second key cost you'll need to know to plan your Kickstarter campaign. To begin, you must decide whether you'll be handing your books yourself or having the POD printer do it for you via drop-shipping. There is a third option, which is to hire a third-party fulfillment company. This is an option to consider if you know you'll be fulfilling orders for hundreds of books. It's generally not necessary for most authors, especially with a first-time campaign.

Handling your books yourself.

If you are planning to autograph your books, include swag, or create fancy book boxes, you will need to have your books sent to you from the printer. This is true whether your books are offset printed or POD.

Once you receive your books, you'll need to process them, package them, and mail the rewards out to individual backers. Don't forget to include your shipping materials. Boxes, packing tape, envelopes, and bubble wrap aren't free.

Drop-shipping.

One of the advantages of POD projects is that you can have the printer—Ingram, Lulu, Bookvault, or KDP—print and mail the books directly to each individual backer. This can save you a lot of time and hassle, but you won't be able to autograph the books or add swag to the package. For the best of both worlds, some authors drop-ship books from the printer and then send signed bookplates and swag separately.

Most offset printers don't drop-ship. These printers need to ship the entire order to one address. If you don't want to personally handle packaging and shipping each book reward, you'll need to hire a third-party fulfillment company. They will receive your boxes of books, package them for each order, and mail them to your backers. These companies charge a fee per order on top of shipping. If your campaign is wildly successful and you're looking at sending out hundreds or thousands of books, a third-party fulfillment company can help preserve your sanity.

Note: Pledge managers, like BackerKit and PledgeBox, do *not* assist with physical fulfillment. They will not package or mail your books for you. There are also no printers "integrated" with Kickstarter. You'll need to figure out how to get your rewards to your backers.

Calculating the postage.

To figure out the cost of mailing out your books yourself, you'll need to know the weight of your packages. A kitchen scale is an essential tool. Don't forget to include the weight of the packing materials and any extra swag you're sending. You also need to know the dimensions of your box. These are often printed on the bottom.

Once you know your weight and the dimensions of your package, calculate the shipping via a free shipping consolidator company. Many authors prefer Pirate Ship, although Easyship and ShipStation are also popular choices. These companies provide discounts on shipping from USPS, FedEx, and UPS. You can pay for and print labels at home, and sometimes even arrange for your boxes to be picked up. Even though these companies cannot further discount USPS Media Mail (the cheapest way of shipping books within the U.S.), you can still pay for and print the labels using these services. If you are only sending books (and possibly paper swag), consider using Media Mail.

If you don't have your books in hand, use a similar-sized book off your shelves to arrive at a ballpark cost. When calculating U.S. shipping, choose a state that's far from your own to get an idea of what your highest shipping costs might be.

Finally, if you are figuring out costs for a campaign that might not ship for several months, be aware that postage costs could rise during the interim. Verify your shipping right before your campaign goes live. You might also want to add a cushion, or consider charging shipping after your campaign ends, via a pledge manager like PledgeBox or BackerKit.

If you are drop-shipping from a POD printer, use their online price calculators to arrive at your shipping costs. Make sure to double-check right before your campaign goes live to see whether prices have changed.

INTERNATIONAL SHIPPING

You don't *have* to offer physical books to international backers. You could choose to leave the rewards shipping on Kickstarter set to U.S. only. Some authors put a note in their campaign asking international backers to send a message if they're interested in getting print books. If there's a supporter in another country who wants to pledge, you can figure out the shipping just to their country and add that into your tiers.

Just be aware you will be leaving money on the table if you don't open your physical rewards to international backers.

One of the things that stops U.S. creators from offering print books outside the U.S. is the cost of overseas shipping. It's much more expensive than we are used to. But international backers are used to paying high shipping costs. Ask any Australian about international shipping to their country—for anything, not just Kickstarter rewards—and you'll be amazed at how much they have to pay.

In addition to high shipping fees, there are often questions about VAT, customs, and overseas taxes. For the most part, these are not as fraught as you might think. Many creators add shipping disclaimers for international backers in their campaign. It's a good idea to make international backers aware they might have to pay additional fees to receive their rewards, and that those fees and taxes will be their responsibility.

The advantage of using a POD printer and drop-shipping your book directly to backers is that most POD companies have printing facilities overseas. Shipping directly from Ingram UK or Bookvault UK to an address in the U.K. can cost the same as, or even less than, sending a book in the U.S. from a U.S. printer. The countries that generally have higher shipping costs are Australia and Canada, so make sure to keep an eye on anything you plan to ship to those destinations. However, if you are using Lulu to print your books, they have facilities worldwide. Although their cost to print is high, their international drop-shipping rates can be amazingly low.

If you are drop-shipping and then sending out paper swag or signed bookplates, don't forget to check the international postage rates. Letters under one ounce are currently $1.50 to send from the U.S. to over 180 countries worldwide. Watch the weight, too. Once your letter goes over one ounce, the postage increases.

If you are not drop-shipping, but are personally sending signed books and swag out to international backers, things get a bit more complicated. Currently the easiest solution is to sign up with Pirate Ship and ask them for the Simple Export Rate option. This is the most competitive rate for overseas shipping. It is only available for U.S. creators, and the package must weigh less than four pounds.

All of the shipping companies help you with customs information and any extra fees you might be responsible for (generally, there are none). They make the process easy.

For packages over four pounds, you'll need to know your box weight and dimensions, and then use one of the shipping consolidator's calculators to see what the costs will be for various destinations.

You can find dummy addresses for international locations online, or look up international headquarters of various companies to get cities and codes to base your pricing on.

Canadian creators shipping from Canada might want to look into companies like Stallion Express and Chit Chats. They provide shipping solutions to the U.S., often cheaper than Canada Post.

PLATFORM FEES

When figuring out your budget, it's essential to take into account two more extra costs. Kickstarter takes 5% of your final funding amount. They will also deduct another 3-8% in credit card fees. This means you will only get around 90% of your final funding raise. Figure 10% in your campaign budgeting and you should be covered.

This means you must add an extra 10% to *all* your pricing on the platform.

Kickstarter does not make a distinction between rewards and shipping when they take their cut. If you charge shipping within your campaign, that amount is added to the backer's pledge. Kickstarter rolls everything into one lump sum (your total funding amount) and take their fees off the top.

Some creators avoid this by charging shipping after their campaign ends via a pledge manager like PledgeBox or BackerKit. Although these companies do not take 10%, there are other costs associated with using them, including credit card fees. If you go this route, you'll need to know what those costs are.

HIDDEN COSTS

When calculating your expenses, don't forget your packaging and shipping materials. Make sure to research in advance the cost of boxes and bubble wrap/crinkle paper/etc. Any extra swag you plan to provide to your backers needs to be figured in. There will also inevitably be items that are damaged in shipping and the potential of lost shipments. Build in some extra room for those losses.

Another hidden cost to take into consideration is taxes. Kickstarter does not submit taxes on your behalf. It does, however, report your campaign funding amounts meeting certain tax thresholds. Taxes are beyond the scope of this book. Consult your CPA about the fascinating topic of state and federal taxes. Find out more at Kickstarter and Taxes — Kickstarter

PROFIT EATERS: SHIPPING, SWAG, AND PRICING TOO LOW

Most well-planned Kickstarter campaigns make a profit. There are, however, a few places where you might cut into your profits or even lose money. If you don't charge enough for shipping, spend recklessly on swag, or don't set your pricing or funding goal high enough, your profit margin will suffer. Remember, once your campaign funds, you are obligated to deliver your rewards. You cannot change or renegotiate the pricing after the campaign is over.

Fortunately, you have control. By doing your research, you should know what to charge without going into the red.

Shipping was covered above. Remember that costs often go up several times a year, so double-check your figures before you launch your campaign.

Swag can be fun to make, but bulky and heavy to ship. Items like mugs are not recommended for Kickstarter campaigns. Lighter, unbreakable items are the way to go. Paper goods like bookmarks, cards, and stickers are excellent, low-cost, easy-to-ship items. They also fit in a letter-sized envelope. This makes it easy to mail goodies to overseas backers.

You also control your campaign funding goal. If you have a high product cost like an offset print run or an audiobook, you need to set your goal high enough to cover the expense. You promised your backers certain rewards. Once your campaign funds, you are required to make your project and send those rewards. For high-expense campaigns, an appropriate funding goal is your escape hatch to keep from going in the red. Set the funding amount you need to create what you've promised, then build an enticing campaign that will ensure you reach that goal.

TAKEAWAY

It's critical to sit down and figure out if you can create your project and make a profit. Whether it's back-of-the-napkin figures or a full spreadsheet, you need to know the basics of your costs. In addition to the above section, there are links in the Resources section to good articles on how to budget your Kickstarter project.

PRICING YOUR REWARDS FOR PROFIT

As a rule of thumb, retail prices are calculated by taking the manufacturing cost (the cost to print your books) and roughly doubling that. You can do the same, or higher, with your swag. You shouldn't be doubling your packing materials, the shipping cost, taxes, or any extra handling fees, but you can pass along those actual costs to the backer.

A reward tier calculation might look something like this:

- Hardcover print cost $15.14. Roughly doubled for retail **$29.99**
- Additional book-related cost (shipping to me from the printer) **$1.42**
- Shipping cost from me to backer (U.S. Media Mail) **$4.62**
- Cardboard mailer to package the book **$0.75**
- Bookmark swag **$1.00**
- <u>Subtotal $37.78</u>
- Total - with 10% Kickstarter and credit card fees **$41.55**

Hardcover tiers on Kickstarter generally are around $40. As you can see, there's not a huge amount of profit in there. Only about $15, if you are including U.S. shipping in the tier price itself. One way creators can recoup a bit more is by charging shipping after the backer has chosen their pledge. This is a good approach, especially if you're shipping out book boxes that include swag, or tracking and insuring all your packages.

There's a balance between charging enough to make a profit, but keeping your reward tiers appealing to backers. Again, check what most creators in your genre are doing.

Fortunately, digital rewards can help a campaign reach better profitability. Digital rewards have a time cost, but no production cost. That extra 90% profit, even on a $5 eBook, can help offset the bigger expenses of your campaign.

TAKEAWAY

Don't be daunted by all the moving parts that go into creating a project. Take it one step at a time, and do your research. You'll be able to hit that launch button knowing your campaign will be profitable. And once you've gone through this process, your next campaign will be much easier to set up.

EXCLUSIVE INTERVIEW WITH ORIANA LECKERT, HEAD OF PUBLISHING AT KICKSTARTER

Oriana Leckert is the Head of Publishing at Kickstarter, where she helps creators bring a marvelous array of literary projects to life. She's written and edited for Vice, MTV News, Slate, Hyperallergic, Gothamist, Atlas Obscura, and many more. Her first book, *Brooklyn Spaces: 50 Hubs of Culture and Creativity* (Monacelli, 2015), grew out of a multi-year project chronicling the rise and fall of under-the-radar creative places across New York City. Follow her at @orianabklyn on most social platforms.

Tell us more about what it means that Kickstarter is a Public Benefit Corporation.

A Public Benefit Corporation is a for-profit company that is obligated to consider how their decisions impact society, not just their shareholders. At Kickstarter, our mission is to help bring creative projects to life, and as it says in our charter, we measure our success as a company by how well we achieve that mission—not by the size of our profits. In practice, this means things like investing in green infrastructure and limiting our environmental impact, donating 5% of our annual after-tax profits to arts and music education and organizations fighting to end systemic inequality, and intentionally building a diverse, inclusive, and equitable organization. For more on the values and commitments we live by as a PBC, see our full charter at kickstarter.com/charter.

What percentage of campaigns are successful in the Publishing category?

As of September 2023, 54% of publishing projects are successfully funded, and that success rate has steadily increased every year since 2015. We're proud of that growth but definitely see an opportunity to do more! One other really important metric is the twenty-five backers threshold. When a project is able to get at least twenty-five backers, it's a signal that the creator is doing the work to reach out to their community and promote their project, and has succeeded in getting beyond just their inner circle. This tells a very different story than the success rate alone: For publishing projects with at least twenty-five backers, an outstanding 83% succeed!

Are there best times of the day and week to launch and end a project?

Yes! We recommend launching early in the day and early in the week, which is when the largest number of people are likely to be online. We recommend ending later in the week and in the afternoon to evening; this is because the final forty-eight hours of any campaign are usually very strong, and you don't want that critical period to land while people are out and about during their weekends. Similarly, be mindful of holidays and seasonality, always aiming to run your campaigns when the majority of your audience will be reachable and attentive.

Is there a certain prelaunch length of time you recommend?

This can vary quite a bit—I've seen creators put up a prelaunch page a whole year before going live! But we tend to see this working the best when the prelaunch period functions as a crescendo into the life of a campaign, building excitement and intensity that culminates in the launch. For this, a week or two is probably plenty of time; much longer than that and it will be difficult to sustain audience enthusiasm, or even their memory. If someone signs up on a prelaunch page and six months go by before they're notified that the campaign has launched, they'll probably have forgotten all about it and may not feel as excited or compelled to back.

What's a good length of time for a campaign to run?

Conventional wisdom here, especially for newer creators, is to run projects for about thirty days, or about four weeks. The majority of a campaign's backings will happen in its first and last week, but having that space in the middle to build enthusiasm, spread the word, get press and amplification, etc., will really help you reach your goal. I've noticed a trend lately of experienced creators shortening that timeline to three weeks or sometimes even less, but the shorter a campaign is, the more important it will be for everything to go right and to happen quickly—the last thing you want is a great piece of press or a cool repost on socials to hit the day after your campaign has closed.

Any advice about making a good video for the project?

Our best tips here are to treat the video like a teaser intended to draw people into the campaign itself, so make sure it's short, bright, and compelling. Our data shows that about 50% of viewers stop watching after one minute, and most of the rest have dropped off after two. So you definitely don't want to expend your time and resources on something long and meandering that most people won't watch anyway! Instead focus just on the highlights of your project—and a view of your lovely face, if you feel comfortable doing so—just enough to make people excited to read through the project page, where you can really tell your whole story.

Are there better months out of the year to run a Kickstarter campaign?

Whenever your community is most reachable, and you've got the most bandwidth to reach them, is the best time to run your campaign. But for some context on Kickstarter as a whole: January and February tend to be pretty quiet, March to June are very busy, July and August are quiet again, September to mid-November are wildly busy, and then things slow down through the holidays and into the New Year. That said, there are pros and cons to being on Kickstarter in both busy and quiet times: when it's busy, there are a lot more active users on the site whose eyeballs your campaign could capture, but there's also much more competition for those eyeballs. A campaign that runs during a slow time can actually have a larger impact because it becomes a big fish in a small pond. Which brings me back to: it's most important to run your campaign at the time that's best for you, your team, and your readership, and then to make the best of whatever is going on on the site as a whole at that time.

Do you have other insights and advice for folks new to the platform? What about experienced creators?

Yes, I'd love to share my top two pieces of advice for new creators. First, if you're thinking about running a campaign, go to the site right now and find five campaigns to back, even for just a dollar or two. Then find and follow those creators out in the world and watch what they do, so you can start to get a sense of how people run their campaigns, how often they communicate with their backers, which rewards are getting the most traction, and things like that. You can also use the site itself as a massive historical database, since every campaign that has ever run is still there in our search results. Looking at lots of projects can help you get a sense of what people in the past have done right and wrong, and then you can borrow all the best ideas you find.

The second most important piece of advice I have is to make sure you're focusing on building community long before you think about launching a project. Everyone thinks about the "funding" side of crowdfunding, but of equal or maybe even greater importance is the crowd. That's specifically what you're doing with this kind of fundraising: figuring out who's in your crowd, how to reach them, and what to offer to make them very excited to support your creative journey.

I know you attend a lot of events! Where can people meet you?

It's true, I'm out in the world a lot! My schedule varies each year but I'm usually at events like Dragon Con, AWP, 20 Books Vegas, NINC, and San Diego and New York Comic Cons. I've also got a unique name and am (sigh) extremely online—you can find me @orianabklyn on most social platforms, and I try to keep my DMs open. If you've got questions for me, please reach out! The best part of my day is getting to talk to authors, illustrators, and other publishing folks about how to raise money to fund their literary dreams.

PART TWO
BUILDING YOUR
CAMPAIGN, STEP BY STEP

CHAPTER 5
START WITH THE BASICS

- Strong Titles
- Strategic Subtitles
- Choose Your Category
- Location
- Brilliant Banners
- Your Video: Share the Excitement
- Funding Fun: How Much to Ask
- Campaign Timing
- Target Launch Date
- Campaign Duration

You've done the hard work of figuring out what project to make. You've worked out your budget and know you won't lose money. Now the fun begins! It's time to roll up your sleeves and head to Kickstarter to create your project. This is my favorite part. (Actually, my favorite part is crossing the funding goal line on a campaign, but we can't get there unless we start at the beginning.)

There is one thing that I recommend all book campaigns have before they launch, and that is the **cover art** for your book. It's essential to show backers what they are pledging money for. People *do* judge books by their covers, and books without covers don't fare very well in any marketplace. With very few exceptions, book projects that don't have cover art in advance struggle to raise enough to meet their funding goal.

I recommend you keep this book (or the Campaign Checklist you'll find at the end) handy as you go to kickstarter.com and begin building your project.

Begin by clicking the "Start a project" link on the upper left, right next to the trusty "Discover" link. This will open up a page with six sections listed across the top—Basics, Rewards, Story, People, Payment, Promotion. We'll go over each of these sections one at a time.

If this is your first campaign, take it slowly. Honestly, pace yourself. There's a lot to do here, and it doesn't need to happen all at once. Sometimes I work on setting up a campaign over the course of a few weeks. After you've built a couple Kickstarter campaigns, it will go faster. My most recent campaign was on the simpler side, and I got most of the creation done in one afternoon. Go at a speed that feels right to you. When your brain gets tired, stop.

Whatever time it takes to build your campaign, make sure you **save often**. I recommend you hit the save button after filling out each field in the Basics section. You never know when you might lose your internet connection—along with the hours of work you just put in.

Like any online platform, Kickstarter can sometimes glitch, too. If you're running into issues or having a hard time adding images, do the following: save the project, refresh the page, then try again.

STRONG TITLES

The first field to fill out in the Basics tab is the title of your campaign. You get sixty characters here, including spaces. Use them to make it very clear what you're offering.

You'll want to explain your core offering, not just put the title of your book. Communicate to passing browsers what your project is. Tell them. Tell them everything. Kickstarter is full of non-book projects. Even if you've put your book in Publishing > Fiction, don't assume that it's obvious your campaign is a book project. Your project will ideally get highlighted on the platform in several different places. Not all of them (Projects We Love, for example) are specific to book-related campaigns.

What to include in your project title.

- The title of your book or series.
- The fact that it's a book! Words like Trilogy, Hardcover, Paperback, etc. can help convey that information.
- The top format you're offering. Here is the order of preference: hardcover, paperback, eBook, and, lastly, audio.
- Anything that makes your campaign special. Deluxe, Special Edition, Exclusive, Collector's Edition, Illustrated, Anniversary Edition, etc.

Here are several of my campaign titles. I made some good choices, and I left some things out I should have included. Learn from my missteps! (Again, the limit for titles is sixty characters.)

Into the Darkwood: Special Hardback Omnibus

This is only forty-three characters. I should have put the word "fantasy" in there as well. I didn't have "book" or "novel" anywhere, but I think "Hardback Omnibus" got the idea across.

The Perfect Perfume & Other Tales - A Steampunk Collection

Fifty-eight characters. While I don't specifically say "book" anywhere, I do have "Tales" and "Collection," which, again, conveys what this project is about. Notice I used the "&" to save a couple of characters. Colons and dashes can be your friends here, too.

The FEYLAND Trilogy 10th Anniversary Special Hardcovers

Fifty-five characters. Again, "Trilogy" and "Hardcovers" are doing the heavy lifting to signal this is a book campaign.

Faerie Hearts: A Romantic Fantasy Collection

Forty-four characters. I maybe could have put "story" in there for "story collection," to make things ultra-clear.

Kickstarter for Authors: Helping Writers Fund and Flourish

Fifty-seven characters, and I really couldn't jam "book" in there anywhere, unless I'd titled it "A book to help writers succeed" or something along those lines. Luckily, the subtitle gives us more characters for communicating the specifics of our project.

The Duke's Christmas: Dainty Paperback Edition

Forty-six characters. I went back and forth about putting the words "romance" or "romantic" in the title, but decided I'd save that for the subtitle.

Elfhame Fantasy Trilogy - Deluxe Collector's Hardcovers (my upcoming project)

Fifty-five characters. I will probably play with this a bit more. There are other words that could go here, including "exclusive" and "foiled." Whatever doesn't make it into the final title will definitely go in the subtitle.

From my study of hundreds (at this point, probably thousands) of campaigns, **I do not recommend the following**.

- Just your book title. "Winterset" doesn't mean anything to a casual browser. "Winterset: Exclusive Epic Fantasy Hardcover" will get the right book backers interested in your project.
- Too many adjectives. Leave those for the subtitle.

- Your author name, unless you have a big fanbase. That's right there on the project page and probably in your URL (if you set that up correctly).
- "Book Two" or onward in a series. Don't give folks an opportunity to bail out or think "well, I don't have Book One, so never mind." Make the title about your series, not an individual book within it. Remember, you will be offering the earlier books in your series as part of your tiers.
- "Audiobook." Don't use this word unless that is the only thing the campaign is about (or the only new format you're offering). Again, don't turn folks away at the door. As mentioned earlier, audiobooks are fourth down on the list of what Kickstarter backers are looking for. If you lead with that, many will assume you're not offering the other formats.

TAKEAWAY

You have sixty characters. Make your title clear, and be obvious about what you're offering.

STRATEGIC SUBTITLES

Kickstarter gives you 135 characters for your subtitle, so you've got a bit more room to get your campaign across here. Use your subtitle for any extra information you couldn't put into the title. I recommend things like your tropes, subgenre, and comp titles (yes, you can do that on Kickstarter). Include anything else specific to your book that will help prospective backers know what you're offering and whether it's something they like. Three-book omnibus, deluxe edition, spicy, sweet, NSFW, etc.

Together, your title and subtitle are indexed into Kickstarter's search engine, so make sure you put in *all* your key elements. Think of your title and subtitle fields like those seven keyword boxes at Amazon. This is where the search is going to draw from, so use it well.

To get the most valuable information into your subtitle, be clever about your character use. Lean on dashes and colons. Leave out that period at the end, if you're out of room.

What to include in your subtitle.

Use as many of the 135 characters as humanly possible. Seriously, reword and rework for maximum usage while still having an appealing flow. You're a writer, right?

- Your specific subgenre, in the title or subtitle.
- Anything extra about what makes your project special or unique.
- Comp titles. I've seen some campaigns do well with those types of comparisons. "Lord of the Rings in Space" etc.
- Your author cred, if that's germane. *NYT* or *USA Today* bestseller adds credibility to your books, but choose wisely. Coming across as egotistical can backfire. "Astonishing book by an incredible new talent" hurts more than it will help.
- If you didn't make it clear in the title what kind of project you're creating (hardcover, graphic novel, children's book, etc.), make sure it's in the subtitle.

Here are the subtitles that I used for those campaigns mentioned above. (Again, 135 characters is the maximum for subtitles.)

Into the Darkwood: Special Hardback Omnibus

From USA Today bestselling author Anthea Sharp, a complete fantasy trilogy of 700 pages packed with magic, romance, and adventure.

One hundred and thirty characters. I used my author name because my Kickstarter profile and vanity URL is set to Fiddlehead Press. This was also my chance to use some "social proof" that my books are appealing to readers with the *USA Today* bestseller title.

Even though I didn't get "fantasy" into the title, I pulled it in here. "Complete" is always appealing to readers.

Tagging the large page count of this omnibus helped make it clear what I was offering. I also included the things readers could expect, like magic, romance, and adventure. Vague, but better than nothing. This was my first campaign, and it was very successful. **Into the Darkwood** funded over $7k for a backlist trilogy in a new hardcover omnibus edition. If I had a do-over, I'd probably try to add the word "elves" in there somehow.

The Perfect Perfume & Other Tales - A Steampunk Collection

From USA Today bestseller Anthea Sharp, nine stories filled with thrilling airships, intrepid heroines, clockwork devices, and more!

One hundred and thirty-two characters. I patterned this one on my first, super-successful campaign, and again put my name and credentials in. "Nine stories" helped fill out what, precisely, was in the Steampunk Collection.

I had fun with adjectives, clearly! Overall, this was a very fun campaign to run. I played up all the Steampunk elements as much as possible. This project funded $5.6k for a paperback edition of backlist stories. Looking back, I might have included a couple comp titles here.

The FEYLAND Trilogy 10th Anniversary Special Hardcovers

What if a high-tech game opened a gateway to the treacherous Faerie Realm? Discover the USA Today bestselling fantasy series today!

One hundred and thirty-one characters. I've used that tagline for the series pretty much forever, and it always pulls readers in, so I used it here to get the idea of the genre mix across. As this was the series I twice hit the USA Today list with, I wanted to lean on that fact here.

In retrospect, I could have used "complete" and maybe even "GameLit" in this subtitle. I could also have added the word "portal" in front of fantasy.

I changed the subtitle a couple times while my campaign was live. I often use "Ready Player One with Faeries" as a comp title, and had that for a while for the second part of the subtitle.

I brought existing fans over to the platform for this, my most successful campaign to date. Funded $18.6k, and I also got to make awesome hardcover editions of my books.

Faerie Hearts: A Romantic Fantasy Collection

Tales of love and adventure set in worlds ranging from Ancient Celtic moors to an enchanted forest, where romance and magic reign.

One hundred and thirty characters. I added the word "Tales" to make it clear that this is a story collection. Just to make *sure* prospective backers understood this was romance, I used the word "love." I launched this campaign right before Valentine's Day, for a bit of seasonal resonance. And again, "romance" in the back part of the subtitle.

I wanted to give a sense of the flavor of the stories, and used words to that effect. All together, I feel I really communicated the "Faerie Tales, romantic stories, Celtic love, fantasy magic" vibe. This is one where my banner integrated with those tropes, as well, making for a very successful combination. This campaign funded at $7.7k for a paperback new release.

Kickstarter for Authors: Helping Writers Fund and Flourish

Proven strategies & insider tips from a platform pro. Best practices and detailed, step-by-step guidance to level up your campaign!

One hundred and thirty-one characters. I worked on this one a LOT, trying to convey everything: my credentials, what kinds of things were inside, and why authors needed this book. I also didn't put "book" anywhere—oops. Could I have done better? Maybe. But as I tell my kid, "Don't let the perfect be the enemy of the good." I could have spent months tinkering with this one, but at some point you just need to get that project launched.

And yes, I still have nerves every time I hit that big green button.

The Duke's Christmas: Dainty Paperback Edition

Sweetness awaits in this Victorian-set tale featuring friends-to-enemies-to-lovers romance, unexpected guests, and holiday delights!

One hundred and thirty-two characters. "Sweet" is used in romance to signal little to no intimate contact between the characters. I wanted backers to know what to expect from this book. The Victorian setting signals it's a historical romance, and I put in a few of the tropes and flavor of the story. Romance without any fantasy/paranormal elements generally doesn't fund particularly high on Kickstarter. With this campaign, I tried to lean harder on the holiday elements and pull back a bit on the romance.

Elfhame Fantasy Trilogy - Deluxe Collector's Hardcovers

Luxe limited/numbered editions, foiled case & custom edges. Dark Elves, an enchanted forest, low-steam cozy romance & fairytale twists.

One hundred and thirty-five characters. The very limit. I will probably keep tweaking this one up until (and beyond) launch. As I get closer to making this campaign live, I'll pay careful attention to what type of wording the super-successful fantasy special edition projects have been using.

For your subtitles, I do *not* recommend the following.

- Repeating anything that's already in your title. Every character is gold. Don't waste it in repetition.
- Being super short. Again, this is keyword gold. Put in the words that people who would support your campaign will be using to search for things they like.
- Using your book tagline unless it's very tropey and descriptive. Don't use something vague like "She wanted to know all the answers…" or anything that will simply make backers scratch their heads, shrug, and move on.

TAKEAWAY

Make your subtitle hooky and interesting, keyword-rich, and as close to the maximum 135 characters as possible.

CHOOSING YOUR PROJECT CATEGORY

Primary category. For almost all book campaigns, Publishing is the best primary category to pick. There are exceptions. If you're making a comic or creating an illustrated art book, you should select Comics or Art as your primary category. Categories are the main way Kickstarter organizes projects. Backers can search categories to find the type of project they are interested in supporting. Be aware that a project can only appear in one category (and associated subcategory) at a time.

Here are the current primary project categories on Kickstarter:

- Art
- Comics
- Dance
- Design
- Fashion
- Film and Video
- Food
- Games
- Journalism
- Photography
- Publishing
- Technology
- Theater

Primary subcategory. Choose the best primary subcategory within Publishing. Most fiction authors go with Fiction. Depending on your book, you might fit better in Anthologies, Young Adult, Children's Books, Nonfiction, or Poetry. If you have a book that crosses subcategory lines—say, an anthology of YA fantasy—then you have options. I recommend you launch with the bigger Fiction subcategory to begin your campaign.

Here are the current Publishing subcategories:

- Academic
- Anthologies
- Art Books

- Calendars
- Children's Books
- Comedy
- Fiction
- Letterpress
- Literary Journals
- Literary Spaces
- Nonfiction
- Periodicals
- Poetry
- Radio & Podcasts
- Translations
- Young Adult
- Zines

In addition to the primary category and primary subcategory, your dashboard shows boxes to select a second category and subcategory. Currently, there is little benefit to doing so. According to Kickstarter support, choosing a second category doesn't put your project into that category on the platform, or even index it in the searches.

Changing categories. Good news! If your campaign fits into several subcategories, you can move around *while your campaign is live.* Put that YA anthology into the Young Adult or Anthology subcategories. If your campaign includes things like Oracle cards along with your book, then you might want to experiment with moving out of Publishing and into Games > Playing Cards for a portion of your campaign's live period.

The category switch happens almost immediately and can help boost your campaign's visibility if you've hit the dead zone. Don't expect an immediate uptick, though. Give your new category a couple days to gain traction before switching it back. And don't abuse this ability. Amazon eventually cracked down on authors' abilities to choose subcategories because people were deliberately putting things in all the wrong places. Luckily, this is a somewhat self-correcting problem on Kickstarter. It's unlikely that backers will respond positively if you list your poetry book in Graphic Novels. But if your book really does cross category lines, experiment with seeing where it might find the best traction.

TAKEAWAY

Whatever primary category and subcategory you choose, that's where your project will display. The second category is currently not a thing. You can switch categories while your project is live. Use this power wisely.

LOCATION

Kickstarter requires you select a location. In the U.S., you will need to type in a city and state. Outside the U.S. you will put in your city and country. Most creators choose their town or nearest big city, but if your project is deeply tied to a locale, consider putting that in as your location. This information is also indexed into the search engine, so whatever you put in will be searchable.

P.S. Don't forget to hit the "save" button regularly!

BRILLIANT BANNERS

One place authors often go wrong on Kickstarter is creating their campaign banner. We're good with words, but aren't necessarily graphic designers. As a result, many authors try to put way too much on their banners, especially words. Kickstarter doesn't recommend you put much, if *any*, text on your banner. Banner images are displayed in several different sizes, most of which are smaller than the one displayed your project page. Your banner needs to be clear and attractive on mobile and when viewed as a thumbnail image.

When making your banner, keep in mind that backers browsing Kickstarter for interesting campaigns will see it at about one-sixth the size it appears on your project page. They don't see your banner at full size unless they click through to your project page, so don't clutter it up by trying to put too much on it. This includes small images of all your rewards as well as unnecessary text. You need a banner that is visually legible and gorgeous even when viewed at a small size.

It is important to check your banner design from your mobile device. A lot of backers access Kickstarter exclusively from their mobiles. Some creators report almost 50% of their supporters backed their projects from a mobile device. Look at your project preview on your phone. Can you tell what you're offering? Is the image clear and enticing?

Your banner always appears on Kickstarter with your title and subtitle displayed either just below or next to it. There's no need to duplicate things like your author name, the words "Kickstarter," etc. Put these things *only* on versions of the banner that you plan to show elsewhere, like your social media and newsletter.

Banner size.

Kickstarter recommends you use a project image that is 1024x576 pixels (16:9 ratio) in size. They take most major image formats, but for best results they recommend JPEG, PNG, GIF, or BMP. The maximum image size is 200 MB.

My recommendations for banners.

The focal point of your banner image should be your book. If your campaign includes a hardcover, make sure you show a 3D hardcover mockup of that format. Tools exist to help you easily create mockups, some of which are listed in the Resources section at the end of this book.

Size the book image up so that the height is almost as tall as the banner. If you're doing a single-book campaign, I recommend you use the other part of your banner to highlight a character, your epic landscape, or some other rich visual. In epic fantasy, the title of the book in its fancy font is another good choice (see the stunning campaigns from Wraithmarked). Although this is text, the title font functions as a graphic element/logo branding.

If your project is for a series, use the book mockup covers in a line, or stacked, or diagonal. Be creative. Just make sure to use those books on your banner in a visually appealing way, along with a contrasting background that conveys a hint of your genre.

What if your book cover isn't ready?

You don't want to launch your campaign without your final book cover. But it's equally important to get your project into prelaunch and start collecting followers. If your cover isn't done, I recommend you make a placeholder banner with a genre-specific background and the book title or series name in a strong, contrasting font. Use this temporary banner to get your campaign into approval and prelaunch. Just make sure your book cover is finished by the time you launch your campaign, and switch to your final banner.

If your cover isn't ready (or even if it is) you can use the fact to create some excitement around your project. Plan a cover reveal! Use your prelaunch page to give fans and prospective backers a first peek at your new cover. This has the added benefit of bringing your readers to Kickstarter, where they can make an account and follow your campaign.

Other considerations.

If you're specifically doing an audiobook campaign and have a strong audio following, the "headphones on a book" graphic does a good job of conveying what's on offer.

Romantic fantasy and paranormal romance campaigns often show the romantic leads on part of the banner. This helps signal the genre to prospective backers.

If you make a campaign video (recommended), be aware that the big green arrow to play the video will be in the exact center of your banner on your project page. Make sure the arrow is not going to cover any key design elements or obscure your gorgeous book cover.

Some creators add a "Funded in X minutes!" or "Project We Love" badge to their banners (if appropriate) after they launch. While Kickstarter doesn't recommend it, extra graphics like these might give your campaign some social proof. On the other hand, they might just clutter up your beautiful graphic. I've seen it both ways. Kickstarter does provide some brand assets, including logos and badges, though they recommend them for use off Kickstarter, not on the platform. You can find a link to those assets in the Resources.

Just as you can change your category while your campaign is live, you can also change your banner after you launch. I recommend you do this if your campaign is in a days-long lull. Sometimes a new image or approach can help get pledges moving again. And especially with first-time campaigns, sometimes the first banner you make doesn't quite hit the mark.

I do not recommend the following for banners.

- Lots of text (or *any* text at all, in most cases).
- An image of your eBook, unless that's the only format you're offering. Show just the most attractive version of your book. Hardcover if you have it. If not, then paperback.
- Every little item in your campaign (sticker, bookmarks, postcards). Don't clutter up your banner.
- Misleading images. If you're not offering a hardcover, don't put one on your banner.

TAKEAWAY

Keep your banner clear, enticing, and attractive even on mobile. Do a Discovery search of Publishing > Fiction campaigns on the platform and skim through projects. Learn from others. Notice what the banners of the well-funding campaigns look like. Trends shift on the platform, and what's considered best practice right now can, and will, change.

VIDEO

A campaign video is not mandatory, though it is recommended. According to Kickstarter, 80% of successful projects have a video.

You don't have to have a video uploaded to get your campaign approved. Sometimes creators don't even add a video until after their campaigns have launched.

When making your video, keep it short and sweet. It should be no more than two minutes, and ninety seconds is even better. Be real, and be enthusiastic about your project. A polished trailer isn't necessary, although some campaigns have used them to good effect. Kickstarter backers are often as interested in the creator of a project as they are in the project itself. They get to be small-scale angel investors. If you are passionate about your book, people will respond to that.

Your video should begin with a quick intro. After you introduce yourself, briefly talk about your project. Then close by asking folks to support. Hold up a copy of your book if you have one. Show and tell is always good. Don't worry about stumbling over words a little. Wear a hat or tiara! (Or not.)

If you really cannot stand the idea of yourself on camera talking for ninety seconds, do an intro, then switch to a voice-over trailer where you show something about your book. Then come back at the very end, ask folks to consider supporting your projects if they love X, Y, and Z, then wave and you're done. Or do a puppet show, or a stop-motion animation. If you're creating an art book or a special edition, or anything graphically appealing, make sure to show off those elements in your video.

Also, don't stress about all this too much. Plenty of prospective backers won't even watch your video. Of those who do, 50% won't continue past the sixty-second mark.

This means you want to have all the information in your video also written clearly in your campaign. Don't say something important in your video that you don't put on your project page. A lot of prospective backers will miss that information if you don't mention it both places.

One final tip: create your video in landscape mode, not portrait. Kickstarter will add black spaces on either side of a portrait aspect ratio, making your video smaller and harder to watch, especially on mobile devices.

TAKEAWAY

Keep your video under two minutes. Be yourself and show what's awesome and exciting about the thing you're hoping to make. Why do *you* love it? Communicate your enthusiasm to prospective backers.

FUNDING FUN

On Kickstarter, if your campaign doesn't reach the funding goal you set by the time your campaign ends, you receive no money for your project. For example, if you set a goal of $5,000 and fund only $4,999, you will get none of that funding raise. For this reason, it's essential to set your funding goal strategically. There's a tricky balance between setting your goal high enough that it covers your costs, and low enough that you don't walk away with nothing.

Fortunately, books are not like many of the other things creators bring to life on Kickstarter. Projects like games, comics, movies, and tech equipment have high up-front costs. If those campaigns don't raise tens of thousands of dollars to cover production, the projects simply cannot be made. The funding goal acts as a safety valve. If a campaign fails to fund, backers and creators aren't left financially committed to a half-funded project that can never be made.

Books, on the other hand, are different. In most cases, authors plan on releasing their book regardless of the outcome of their Kickstarter campaign. It's usually not a "Kickstarter or no book" proposition. A lot of the work is already done in preparation for a retail release. You've probably already paid for editing and covers. When you create a Kickstarter campaign, you need your funding to cover the specific costs of producing and delivering the rewards you're promising to backers. The leftover profit can go toward defraying the sunk publishing costs, but your retail release profits will be doing the same. It's not necessary, and maybe not even reasonable, to expect your campaign to pay back all your costs. Because of this, many book campaigns tend to set a lower funding goal.

Think about it. Both POD and eBooks are ultimately scalable. You can create as many as you have pledges for. If your reward tiers are calculated to make a 40%-80% profit on each book (depending on format), then that margin exists whether you have twenty backers or twenty thousand. Your success isn't dependent on a huge funding raise. Whether you hit $500 or $5000, each pledge will be profitable. This is why I often say your funding goal is a floor, not a ceiling.

Setting an attainable funding goal.

If you are creating a POD book, it's recommended you set your funding goal around $500. This is a threshold most book projects using best practices will be able to meet. As long as you price your rewards correctly, you should be able to walk away from a funded Kickstarter with money in your pocket. If you are creating an eBook-only project in a non-fantasy genre, I recommend you consider a funding goal below $500.

Again, remember that your funding goal is a floor. Setting it at $500 doesn't stop you from possibly funding much higher. When studying campaigns on Kickstarter, don't forget to look at the original funding goal. Many of those $10k+ campaigns started with a very modest goal.

Setting a smaller goal also gives your project a better chance of reaching its funding within the first few days after you launch. Here are the advantages of funding earlier in your campaign.

- Reduced stress. Launching your first Kickstarter is hard enough without having to bite your nails every

day for three weeks worrying if you'll make your
funding goal.

- Success builds success. Backers like to jump aboard a
campaign that's already funded, since it means the
project will definitely be happening. Raising 300% (or
more) over your funding goal isn't a detriment.
- Initial velocity can help carry you further, getting
your campaign seen in more places on the Kickstarter
platform.
- Funding early gives you a chance to celebrate with
the backers who helped get you to that point! Don't
forget the social aspect of running a campaign. It
gives you an opportunity to let your early supporters
know they are important and appreciated. Everyone
loves a win.

Some creators use the extra profit from a well-funded
campaign to upgrade their product and add bonuses for their
supporters. These are called stretch rewards, and there's a
section about them further on.

There are some arguments to be made about perceived value,
or looking a little silly if you set a $500 goal for a project that
funds well into the five figures. Once you have some experience on the platform, you can bring more nuance to setting
your funding goal. Now that I've run several Kickstarter
campaigns, I feel comfortable setting the goal for my POD
fantasy book projects at $1k. For first-time POD campaigns,
unless you know you'll be bringing hundreds of fans to the
platform to support you, start with that $500 goal.

When to set a higher funding goal.

If your project has higher up-front costs, then you need to take those into account when setting your funding goal. Your goal needs to be high enough to cover the cost of what you are making. If your project needs funds for an offset print run, to pay anthology contributors, commission art for a graphic novel, or hire an audiobook narrator, make sure you can cover enough of your production costs. You are responsible for delivering the rewards you are promising your backers. You don't want to lose money doing so.

Set your funding goal to the minimum you need to success-fully get the rewards into backer's hands. Don't go into the red on your rewards.

You might also have a project that you feel isn't worth your time and energy unless it funds to a certain level, regardless of your costs. Sometimes it might be better to have no obliga-tion to complete a project unless it's worth your financial while. Still, keep in mind there are intangible benefits to running a Kickstarter. Reaching a new audience, gaining experience on the platform, upping your marketing skills, etc., all have value.

TAKEAWAY

Starting with a smaller funding goal doesn't mean you can't end big. It's a floor, not a ceiling. That said, if you really need to raise a certain amount to make your project happen, set the goal for what you'll need.

CAMPAIGN TIMING

When should your campaign start and end? How long should it last?

The first question is relatively easy to answer. Launching your campaign earlier in the week (Monday or Tuesday) and ending it later in the week (Thursday) is generally recommended. Avoid major holidays and weekends if you can, as Kickstarter tends to see less backer activity on those days. That said, if your situation requires you to start or end on a weekend, do it.

Launch your campaign in the morning and end in the afternoon or evening (U.S. time zones). You want to make your campaign live when most of your target audience is awake.

Choosing the end point of your campaign is less straightforward. If you end on a Friday after business hours, that could delay your payment. Kickstarter releases campaign funds (minus their cut and credit card fees) to your bank exactly fourteen days after your project ends. If this falls on a weekend, your bank might not post the money to your account until the following Monday. Or Tuesday, if Monday is a bank holiday.

Some creators find ending right before the end of the month results in more errored pledges, since backers might be low on money and are waiting for their paychecks to come in. I wouldn't go to great lengths to avoid this, however, as the evidence is anecdotal.

One other thing to consider is the timing of the emails Kickstarter sends to people who are following, but have not yet backed, your campaign. The platform notifies followers forty-eight hours and eight hours before your campaign ends. If your project finishes at seven a.m., many prospective backers will be asleep and will miss that final opportunity to support your campaign.

How many days should your campaign run? The platform allows creators to run a campaign anywhere from one to sixty days. Those are the outer extremes. Kickstarter recommends that projects run for around thirty days, but other metrics suggest there is a sweet spot at seventeen to twenty-four days.

For a first-time project, I recommend you stay within that optimum three-week window. Running a campaign can be taxing. It's an emotional roller coaster, and not being on that ride for a full month will help save your sanity. There are, however, some creators who aren't very hands-on during their Kickstarter campaigns. For them, a long campaign duration may work just fine. You might find that you're one of those rare types who can set up a campaign and then step back for weeks at a time. If so, then do what works best for you.

Typically, funding on Kickstarter usually starts with a quick rise, flattens out for the majority of your campaign, and then ends with an uptick. That is the most common funding pattern. It's a mistake to think that if you can raise a certain amount in thirty days, you can double that with a sixty-day campaign. That's not how Kickstarter works. You will probably gain a little more funding, but a longer campaign mostly means a longer flat period in the middle, where you will gain and lose pledges in a two-steps-forward, two-back funding dance.

Remember the comparison of your Kickstarter campaign to running a sales booth or hosting an online party? How long can you sustain that energy? Starting with a shorter campaign will give you a feel for how you, personally, deal with the ups and downs, the backer interactions, managing stretch rewards, etc. A Kickstarter campaign works as a concentrated promotional burst. Think about what feels reasonable for you in terms of sustaining enthusiasm for your project.

I personally set my campaign lengths anywhere from fifteen to thirty days, depending on the scale of the project. Bigger ones, like my Feyland tenth anniversary editions, got a full four weeks. Single paperbacks of a short story collection run for closer to sixteen days.

TAKEAWAY

Plan your campaign duration for somewhere between two and four weeks for a first-time campaign. Shorter campaigns help retain a sense of urgency and encourage backers to act quickly due to the short time frame. Once you've got a project or two under your belt, you'll have the experience to decide if you want to experiment with longer or shorter campaign length.

TARGET LAUNCH DATE

The launch date is an optional field. Whatever date you enter is just for your own informational purposes. As authors, we're used to setting up preorders for our books on the retailers, but the Kickstarter platform doesn't work the same way. Setting a target launch date doesn't mean your campaign is going to go live on that specific day. Kickstarter will never auto-launch your campaign. You must manually click the big green button to make your campaign live.

The target launch date only exists to give you, the creator, an idea of what you need to have completed to meet your target date. Kickstarter gives you a timeline to get your campaign through their required steps before you launch. But that date isn't set in stone. It's not set anywhere, except in your own mind.

In fact, Kickstarter's suggested timeline can be a little misleading. It doesn't take into account your prelaunch period, which I recommend be two weeks, minimum.

CAMPAIGN DURATION

The campaign duration section gives you two options. Option one is to set a fixed number of days for your campaign. Option two is to end the campaign on a specific date and time. You can only choose one.

Fixed number of days. This is a very literal field. If you say seventeen days, then your campaign will close exactly seventeen days, to the minute, after you hit the green launch button. I don't advise you do this. The best practice is to launch your campaign in the morning, and end it later in the day.

End on a specific date and time. Get your calendar out. Take the date you plan to launch, and figure out when in the following seventeen to twenty-three days you'd like to end your campaign. Check to avoid U.S. holidays. Once you've chosen your date, now pick a time later in the day. Your end date and time cannot be changed once you launch, so choose wisely.

TAKEAWAY

There is no "one perfect answer" for when to launch and end your campaign. I've launched successful projects on Monday, Tuesday, Wednesday, and Friday. I've ended on every day of the week except the weekend. If your timing/life/energy dictates you run a ten-day campaign, do it. If you have to launch on a Sunday night and end on a Monday morning, do that. Picking optimum launch and end times can help your campaign succeed, but plenty of projects with less-than-optimal times do just fine.

A final note about the Basics.

Once your campaign launches, you cannot change the end date or the funding goal. Everything else remains editable. You can swap out a different banner, add or delete your video, reword your title and subtitle, and move your project into a different category or subcategory. The only irrevocable mistakes you could make here are setting your funding goal too low and losing money on reward fulfillment, or way too high and having nothing to show if your campaign ends unsuccessfully.

CHAPTER 6
REWARDS AND ADD-ONS

- Rewards Best Practices
- Building Your Rewards
- Title
- Amount
- Reward Tier Image
- Description
- Items
- Contents
- Shipping
- Estimated Delivery
- Project Quantity
- Time Limit
- Add-ons

In this next major dashboard section, you'll build out the reward tiers and add-ons for your campaign. What wonderful rewards are you offering your backers?

REWARDS BEST PRACTICES

Each reward tier and add-on has a number of fields to fill out, including the pricing, the description, the items you're offering within the tier, and whether or not you're charging shipping. In addition to filling out your tiers, you'll need to decide how many tiers to offer and follow some general pricing guidelines.

How many tiers should you offer?

Limit yourself to a maximum of ten reward tiers. Too many options are confusing (it's called choice overload). If your tier structure is overly complex, you will lose supporters because picking a tier takes too much effort.

You can have a successful campaign with very few tiers. I've seen them do quite well. Wraithmarked (a company that has created many successful book projects on Kickstarter) often offers only two reward tiers: a foiled bookmark at a lower pledge level and a deluxe hardcover at a higher amount.

Combine rewards wisely.

Backers can only pledge for one reward tier. Tiers cannot be added together. Therefore, you have to anticipate the types of reward packages that will appeal to different kinds of backers. There are supporters who want just the books. There are others who want swag, and your backlist, and a Zoom meeting, and a signed edition of your book. Don't break those items into separate tiers. It's better to combine them in a high-level superfan tier, instead.

Offer add-ons.

One way to let your backers have everything they might want is to put items in add-ons instead of (or addition to) the reward tiers. Unlike reward tiers, backers can select multiple add-ons. They can mix and match to their heart's content.

Your backlist books make perfect add-ons and can help increase your funding by giving backers more to pledge for.

If you'd like to offer things like swag packs in your campaign, consider whether those might be better as add-ons instead of taking up a reward tier spot.

We'll go deeper into this topic in the add-ons section. For now, it's enough to know that you don't need to create a tier for every possible combination of rewards.

General pricing guidelines.

Before you begin, you must have a good idea of how to price your rewards to make a profit.

But remember, you're also trying to build a base of supporters for future Kickstarter campaigns. Offer nice things to backers at prices where you make a decent return, and also make sure your rewards are more or less what other creators are asking. Kickstarter backers aren't looking for deep discounts, but they know when a creator is overcharging for rewards. They will not support a campaign that feels like a money grab. If you need to price your tiers higher than the norm, have a clear justification and communicate it well.

If you're offering some items in your reward tiers that are already available on retailers, don't inflate your Kickstarter prices. If your eBooks are $5 at retailers, don't ask for $7 on Kickstarter. In fact, I recommend you keep the pricing the same but add value. Include something extra that won't increase your shipping or production cost, like bonus scenes or digital artwork. You want backers to support you on Kickstarter, not just purchase from the retailer.

Adding tier items.

There are two ways to add items to your reward tiers. You can click on the word "Items" on the Rewards and Add-ons page, and add everything you plan to offer in your tiers, one by one. Alternatively, you can add items during the process of creating each reward tier. This will automatically add them to the "Items" list.

Whether you add items as you create the reward tiers or list them all up front via the items option is up to you. Either way, when you have finished making your reward tiers, you'll have an itemized list of everything you're offering to backers. At fulfillment time, the Kickstarter dashboard will tell you exactly how many of each item you will need to fulfill all the pledges.

For each item, use a clear description of what you're offering and include an image of just that item. "Elfhame – Hardcover Edition," for example, with an image of the hardcover mockup on a white background.

Remember, ITEMS are not tiers or add-ons. They are just the name of the thing (and image of the thing) that you will be adding to the reward tiers and add-ons. Once you add them into tiers or add-ons, you will have the ability to add more description.

BUILDING YOUR REWARDS

For a first-time campaign, I recommend you start simple. You might have three or four tiers: the eBook, the paperback, the hardcover, and the hardcover with swag. Don't force people to pledge for an expensive swag tier in order to get your book. While many Kickstarter backers love extra goodies like bookmarks and stickers, there are plenty that don't. Even with a swag-heavy campaign, I recommend a "no frills" tier for your physical books. That reward level can be completely plain, or you could include something simple, like a bookmark, that's included with all physical tiers at no extra cost.

For authors in Kindle Unlimited, Amazon's TOS does not allow you to sell your eBook elsewhere while you have it in the Select program. This includes Kickstarter. Either forgo an eBook tier, or remove your book from KU while your Kickstarter is live.

Some authors have a free first-in-series eBook. If you do, either offer it in a $1 tier, potentially with another digital reward (plus add it to all other tiers), or raise the price on the retailers before you run your campaign.

If you are offering both digital and physical copies of your book, you'll need to decide if you want to include your eBook for free with the print books, or charge slightly more. Again, don't make backers pledge for something they might not be interested in. If the only way to get your hardcover is by paying extra for the eBook, you will end up with people who decide not to support your campaign at all.

Many authors provide the eBook for free as a perk to backers supporting the campaign. Other authors create a slightly more expensive tier for the print plus eBook. As always, study the campaigns in your subgenre to see what the successful campaigns are offering. (And what the backers are supporting, since it's not always the tiers you might expect.)

TITLE

Be clear about what the reward is. If you're offering an eBook, name your reward with the book title and format. For example, "Elfhame – eBook." For my first few campaigns, I used cute names like "Wildflower" and "Forest Explorer" for my reward tiers. While that can be fun and add flavor to a campaign, I now favor clarity in naming the tiers. Especially if you have a lot of them.

You have a forty-character limit for tier titles. Be concise.

AMOUNT

This is the dollar figure you're asking backers to pledge for your items. Here are some ballpark figures for current (fall 2023) reward tier pricing on Kickstarter. You can only enter whole dollar amounts in this field, not cents. Round up that $4.99 eBook to $5.

- Digital books - $5-$15 for a single book ($5-10 is the norm).
- Audiobooks - $10-$25. $15 is currently the most successful tier price for audio.
- Paperbacks - $20-$35 (depends on whether shipping is included, page count, etc.).
- Hardcovers - $35-$50+ (again, whether shipping is included, if it's a big omnibus, if there are exclusive illustrations, etc.).

- Deluxe Special Edition Hardcovers - Anywhere from $55 up to $100+. There are so many factors here, including how fancy the edition is, whether it's an omnibus, etc. Study the special edition market in your subgenre to see what the normal tier range is and what special features are being offered for the price.

The range of prices above depend on whether you're including U.S. shipping in the total cost of the reward. Many creators like to include shipping. That way there's no added shipping charge that pops up after backers make their pledge. At least not to backers within the U.S.

How to include U.S. shipping in your tier cost. When you did your budgeting, you figured out the cost to mail your rewards within the U.S. Take the most expensive option for the items in your tier (shipping to a faraway state, for example) and add that to the reward tier's price. For example, if your paperback costs $8 to print (making the retail price $16) and $9 to ship, then your tier price with U.S. shipping included would be $25. Later, when you get to the shipping portion of creating the tier, set the U.S. shipping cost to $0, because you've already included in the overall reward tier price.

Still not sure how to price your reward tiers? Go to Kickstarter and find the successfully funded fiction campaigns in your genre. Take a look at the tiers. These are listed on the right-hand side of the campaigns on desktop, or via the rewards tab on mobile. Look at the reward pricing, and even more importantly, **look at the number of backers who have pledged to each specific tier.** That tells you what people are going for. A campaign might be offering a paperback for $50, but that doesn't mean backers are supporting at that level. Or they might be, if it's an eight-hundred-page omnibus with a foiled cover and color interior illustrations. You will only be able to tell if the tier pricing is working by seeing which tiers backers are supporting. And even more importantly, which ones they are not.

International creators have the added challenge of dealing with fluctuating currency rates. Kickstarter does not allow you to use anything but your home currency when setting pricing. Make sure you double-check the rates to U.S. dollars right before you launch. Backers will see your currency displayed on the reward tiers, but Kickstarter adds the approximate U.S. value in smaller text below. If you live in a country where your prices will look high to U.S. backers (New Zealand and Australia, for example), make sure to make a note in your campaign about the currency exchange rate.

REWARD TIER IMAGE

This is different from the image of the individual items in a tier. If your reward tier includes multiple books, create a graphic showing all of them. If you are offering only one item in the tier, however, you can use the individual item graphic.

Your reward tier image should be a clear, uncluttered picture of the main item or items that you are offering. If there are three hardcovers, use an image with three hardcover mock-ups. However, resist the urge to put every piece of swag in the picture. Reward tier images appear at a small size. Make sure you check them on your mobile device to see if they are legible.

Each image must have a 3:2 ratio, be no smaller than 348x232 pixels, and no larger than 200 MB. You can upload most major image formats, including JPG, PNG, GIF, TIFF, or BMP file types.

DESCRIPTION

Put a brief yet enticing description of your tier items in this field. Do not put the full product blurb. Again, keep in mind this will be shown fairly small on the Kickstarter site. When building your tiers, highlight the newest item first. For example, if your first tier is an eBook and your second tier is the eBook plus paperback, list and describe the paperback first, and then the eBook.

Kickstarter used to auto-populate a bullet-point list of each included item by name in the reward tier display. Now they only list the number of items without any description. You can still manually add a bullet point list to make it easy for prospective backers to see what items are in your tier. Paste in something like the following:

- Elfhame Hardcover
- Elfhame eBook
- Foiled postcard art
- Heart of the Forest bonus eBook

ITEMS

This is where you add each individual item that will be part of the reward tier. If you created the full Item list earlier, then simply choose which ones are part of the current tier. Otherwise, add each one as a "new item" as you build your reward tier. Make sure the item description is clear and that you include an image of the item on a white or transparent background.

The list of items can be rearranged by dragging to change the order.

You can duplicate a reward tier and use it as a starting point for your next tier. I do this with each of my digital rewards. Then, once I have a physical reward tier set up, I duplicate that one and refine it for each physical tier. When you duplicate, every field is copied. Double-check everything, especially the shipping, to make sure it's correct for the new reward tier. You don't want to end up charging the single-paperback shipping price for your multi-book hardback tiers.

CONTENTS

Here, Kickstarter is asking what type of goods you are offering—digital only, physical only, or a mix of both.

For physical rewards, click "yes" to the question about whether backers will receive any physical goods. Kickstarter will automatically code this in the back end of their system. When you send your post-campaign survey to backers (which is sorted by individual tier), backers of all physical tiers will be required to put in their mailing address.

If you're including eBooks or other digital items along with your physical ones, choose the "physical and digital" option.

If you click "yes" on the physical goods question for a digital-only tier, this might annoy backers who pledged for digital items. Their survey from Kickstarter will require them to fill out their mailing address, even though it's not necessary to deliver their rewards. Mark digital-only rewards appropriately.

SHIPPING

You have four options here. "Ships to anywhere in the world," "Ships to certain countries," "Local delivery," and "Digital rewards (no shipping)." If you are shipping any physical rewards, you need to choose one of the first two options.

Ships to anywhere in the world. This option allows for different shipping costs. You can set some specific countries and then put in a general "rest of the world" cost for everywhere else. I don't generally recommend you choose this option. It's difficult to figure out one shipping cost for most of the world. Only select this option if you plan to use a third-party pledge manager to calculate shipping post-campaign (although I think the next option is a better choice). If you plan to use a third-party pledge manager for shipping, leave the shipping costs here set to zero.

Warning: Kickstarter has a bug in this section. It is possible to have reward tiers marked as only digital goods and accidentally select "Ships to anywhere in the world." Don't do this. If you do, your backers will be required to fill in their mailing address to complete their Kickstarter surveys even though they chose only digital rewards. Some backers abandon their surveys instead of giving out personal information that's not relevant to the reward they selected.

Ships to certain countries. This option allows you to set the U.S shipping, and also add shipping for individual countries. Many creators add the U.K., the EU, Canada, and Australia.

You can add shipping to other countries during the campaign. I've had backers from Switzerland request shipping and have added it for them. "Ships to certain countries" is also the best choice for creators who decide to hire third-party pledge-management companies to charge shipping after the campaign ends, as it limits the countries to the ones you've selected.

U.S. shipping. If you already calculated the cost of U.S. shipping and included it within your tier pricing, leave the U.S. shipping set to zero. If you don't, the backer will be charged double for shipping (once within the tier, and again after they pledge). If you did **not** include U.S. shipping within the pricing of your tier, then enter the U.S. shipping cost here. When a backer selects this reward, the shipping cost is added to the total price of their pledge, increasing it.

International shipping. For shipping to other locations, (U.K., EU, AU, CA, etc.), add those countries and enter your calculated shipping costs for each one.

But! If you've already included an amount for U.S. shipping within your reward tier pricing, you'll want to credit that amount toward international shipping. For example, if you determined that shipping your book to Canada will cost $20, but you already are charging $9 worth of shipping within the tier (for the U.S.), then subtract that $9 from the Canadian shipping, for a final amount of $11. Otherwise, you will be double-charging your backers for a portion of the shipping cost.

If you plan to charge shipping after-the-fact with a third-party pledge manager, leave your shipping at $0.

Pledge managers help you calculate and collect shipping from your backers once your campaign is over. These third-party tools are extra work to set up and have fees. I personally have never used a pledge manager, but there are some advantages to doing so, which are discussed later.

Never try to collect shipping by yourself after your campaign ends. That is a recipe for disaster.

Local pickup. Choosing this option will automatically add another tier to your campaign. This can clutter your project with too many reward tiers and be confusing to backers. In addition, arranging meetups with local supporters, even if they are friends and family, can be complicated and frustrating. Generally, this option isn't recommended unless you have a big in-person event or an enormous local fanbase.

Digital reward (no shipping). Use this for your digital-only reward tiers.

ESTIMATED DELIVERY

Be realistic about how long it will take to get rewards to backers. You're going to need to wait until Kickstarter releases your funds. You'll need to send out backer surveys and have them returned. You'll need to package and ship physical books and resolve shipping any problems or delays. You'll be doing all this while weathering any unexpected surprises that crop up in your personal life.

Most creators wait until the Kickstarter campaign funds are deposited into their bank account (about two weeks after the campaign ends) before delivering any rewards.

Even if you have digital items ready to go the moment the campaign is over, I recommend you build in a full month to deliver those rewards. You never know when you might have something come up in your life that will delay your ability to fulfill your campaign rewards.

For physical rewards, I recommend you set the delivery date two months out from the end of your campaign, provided your book is written, formatted, and ready to go. It's fine to deliver rewards early. Under-promise and over-deliver is always a good strategy. Just make sure you build in a safety cushion in case of delays. There can be delays on the backer side, too. Some backers don't return their surveys right away, and you won't have the information you need to deliver their rewards until they do.

If your campaign included ordering an offset print run for your books, factor in even more time. Printers often run into delays. If your books are shipping from a printer overseas, shipping delays are inevitable.

A good rule of thumb for setting your estimated delivery is to figure out your most realistic timeline. Then add another month.

PROJECT QUANTITY

You have two options in the project quantity box, limited and unlimited. If your reward tier might run out, choose limited. Maybe you only have the materials for five fancy book boxes, or ten special pins, or you'd like to offer the first few numbered editions of your book at a higher price point. Set the reward limit amount here in the project quantity. Once that number has been reached, Kickstarter marks those reward tiers as no longer available to back.

You can adjust the limited amounts upward after your campaign launches. For example, you discover you can make two more fancy book boxes. Just note that you can't decrease the amount you've offered.

Use the unlimited setting if you can make as many rewards to fulfill this tier as you have backers for. EBook and POD books are generally unlimited. If you are doing an offset print run, you can usually add to your order amount from the printer.

TIME LIMIT

You can set your reward tier to expire after a certain time. Do that here with the time limit setting.

Use this feature to create limited-time early-bird rewards. A discount or added bonus can give you a strong campaign launch and help you reach your funding goal early. Most authors let their early-bird rewards expire anywhere from twenty-four to forty-eight hours after their campaign goes live.

Some creators limit the number of early-bird rewards. In general, though, early birds are more effective as time-limited tiers. You want to reward early backers. If people show up the first day to make their pledge and you've already run out of rewards, that can leave a bad taste in backer's mouths.

When you set up a time-limited reward, it doesn't display correctly on your campaign preview. Don't worry if it doesn't look right. Once you launch, everything should be correct.

More on early-bird rewards.

Some creators offer special early deals to entice backers to pledge right away. This can be a discount on one or more of your tiers, or an additional bonus added to certain tiers. Create them as described above. They're not required, but they can be a tool to help give you a strong launch and reward your early supporters.

To discount a tier, duplicate the one you'll be discounting, put in the lower price, and then give it a time or item limit. Remember that Kickstarter backers aren't necessarily looking for cheap deals. I wouldn't advise anything over 5-10% as a discount.

You can also add extra goodies to a duplicated tier, and again, either time- or item-limit it.

One of the things I sometimes do is provide a little something to all backers who pledge in the first day, or forty-eight hours. You could also do a "first fifty backers" reward or something similar. I usually add a bookmark or custom digital wallpaper. I've seen creators offer stickers, or a bonus eBook or short story. The all-backers type of early bird is one you'll need to hand-track, but it's not that hard. Kickstarter numbers backers as they pledge. If you're rewarding the first X number of backers, then make a note that folks 1-X get the goodie. If you're doing pledges within the first twenty-four hours, note which backer number you're on when you hit that deadline. Make sure you remember at fulfillment time what the extras are that you've promised your early backers!

Other important things to know about reward tiers.

According to Kickstarter, the most popular reward tier pledge is $25. Make sure you have something to offer in that sweet spot.

Reward tiers are shown on your project page according to the pricing, ranked from least expensive to most. If you have two reward tiers at the same price (not recommended—that could be confusing), the newest one is listed second.

After you launch your campaign and someone pledges to a reward tier, you can no longer change that tier. There are three exceptions: increasing the number of limited rewards, adding a new country for shipping, or changing the image. Other than that, your tier is locked. If no one has pledged, however, you can change it all you like.

You can add new reward tiers while your campaign is live.

If you realize you've made a mistake, you can "retire" a reward tier. You'll still be obligated to provide backers of that tier the items they pledged for, but you won't have to worry about new people pledging. To close a tier, set the project quantity to the amount backers have already pledged for. The tier will then show at the bottom of your rewards as no longer available. If no one has pledged, however, simply delete the problem tier.

Including backer names in your book.

Adding backer names as part of a tier (or stretch reward) can be a great incentive for people to pledge to your campaign. However, you might have a tight turnaround in order to get your book into production. Set a deadline for backers to respond with how they want their name to appear. Some creators make a Google Form and send the link to backers after the campaign ends, with a forty-eight-hour deadline. If they don't get back to you within that time, their names will not be in the backer thank-you section of the book.

Make sure to leave a text field for backers to note how they'd like their name to appear. It's often not their Kickstarter handle. Give them the option to opt-out entirely, too. Not everyone wants to be included (though most do).

ADD-ONS

Add-ons are a great way to make your campaign more profitable. Once a backer has pledged for a reward tier, they will be taken to the add-on section of your campaign. There, they can choose additional items to add to their reward package. Here are some of the things you can offer in your add-ons.

- Your backlist books!
- A video chat with the author.
- Swag, either separately or in swag packs.
- Extra copies of your main offerings (if someone wants to buy a second copy as a gift).
- Items from previous campaigns.
- Classes, critiques, workshops.
- Anything else you can dream up that will add value to your campaign.

Since backers cannot access the add-ons section until they have made a reward pledge, sometimes authors create a "build your own rewards" tier for $1. This allows backers to access the add-ons and choose their preferred options a la carte, instead of pledging for one of the bigger reward tiers.

Creating an add-on is almost identical to creating your reward tiers. There is one extra field, which limits the quantity of the add-on per backer. For example, if you only want backers to be able to get two fancy bookmarks, you can set that in the "backer quantity" field. This field defaults to 10 if you don't input a number.

There is one essential thing to keep in mind about add-ons, and that is the interplay of rewards and add-ons. **Backers of digital-only tiers cannot access any physical add-ons.** Physical backers can access both.

How can authors accommodate backers who support the eBook but want to add physical swag to their pledge?

There are three ways, all of which are a little cumbersome.

The first is to create a $1 "build your own" tier, and make sure to mark it as a physical reward. You will need to include an "item" in the tier. Something like "my thanks" or a free short story are good options. Then make sure your rewards are available in the add-ons section.

The second is to mark your eBook reward tier as a physical reward. This allows eBook backers to access physical add-ons. The disadvantage is that it forces all backers of that tier to fill in their mailing address, even if they don't select a physical add-on. This is not ideal. Many backers will not want to give their home addresses for rewards that are digital-only.

Your third option to allow digital backers to get the physical swag is to create a new reward tier. Make an eBook plus physical swag tier and mark it as a physical item. This has the disadvantage of cluttering up your reward tiers with yet another choice.

Important things to know about add-ons.

Just like the reward tiers, once a backer has pledged for an add-on, you can't change it, other than adding shipping, increasing the backer limit amount, or changing the image. You can create a new add-on at any time during your campaign.

While you are building your campaign, the dashboard shows ALL the additional items that can be added-on to your campaign. Don't fret about that showing in the tiers. While it will be clear to backers what they can and cannot add on, the reward tiers won't be as cluttered up as they appear to you on the dashboard.

Final thoughts about reward tiers and funding.

There is a direct correlation between your average pledge amount and reaching your funding goal. If you have a goal of $500 and your *average* pledge is $15, then you will need to have thirty-four backers to reach your goal. If you can increase the average pledge by offering high-end rewards and enticing add-ons then the number of backers you need goes down. Boost the average pledge to $25 and now you only need twenty supporters, give or take.

If you set a high funding goal but only have low-dollar rewards, you'll have an uphill battle to reach your funding goal unless you know you can bring in a swarm of backers to support your campaign. Set your funding, reward tiers, and expectations appropriately.

CHAPTER 7
STRETCH REWARD STRATEGIES

- Stretch Rewards
- Stretch Goals
- Setting Up Your Stretches
- Flash Rewards
- Backer Perks

Stretch Rewards, Stretch Goals, Flash Rewards, and Backer Perks: What are they and why should you use them?

For years, Kickstarter creators have been using smart strategies to keep momentum going in their campaigns and to reward backers. Stretch rewards, stretch goals, and flash rewards unlock bonuses once certain campaign milestones have been reached. Those, plus backer perks like a new set of bonuses every week, are a great way to reward backers for pledging early and staying in the campaign for the duration.

While none of these strategies are required, they can certainly help your campaign and delight your backers. If you're considering using one of these strategies for your first project, I recommend you start with stretch rewards.

STRETCH REWARDS

Stretch rewards are extra bonuses and goodies that a creator adds to the campaign after the initial funding goal has been met. Projects with lower funding goals sometimes reach those goals quickly, within days or even hours. Stretch rewards help keep a sense of urgency and momentum in your campaign once you've funded.

Although many creators incorporate stretch rewards into their campaigns, these rewards are not an official part of the Kickstarter dashboard. You'll need to personally keep track of the unlocked stretch rewards and make sure backers receive them. Keep a spreadsheet. For the most part, this will be as easy as remembering to include a bookmark with every physical book or provide all backers with a link to download their digital wallpapers or bonus story.

Stretch rewards serve a number of purposes. They keep new backers coming in with the promise that the campaign will continue to get even better than it already is. They reward your current backers with extra goodies and give them a reason not to cancel their pledges. They give you mini goals to shoot for once you're funded and something to post about on social media, especially when your campaign momentum slows. Finally, stretch rewards allow you to add drama and flair to a campaign.

A stretch reward works like this: the creator sets a pledge goal —usually a dollar figure, though it could also be a certain number of backers—and when that goal is reached, a new reward is unlocked. Campaigns often offer from two to ten (or more) stretch rewards. The number of rewards depends on funding velocity (slower-moving campaigns usually unlock fewer rewards) and also how many extras the creator wants to manage.

Stretch rewards are not something you charge backers for once you reach them. They are a free thank-you bonus to everyone for helping support your campaign. Because of this, you need to plan your rewards to make sure they don't eat into your profits.

One way to stay in the black is to build the cost of your stretch rewards into your tiers, within reason. If you're planning to include a bookmark with all pledges, and have already priced that out and added it into the reward cost, consider holding it back as a stretch reward. If you're making bonus stickers to include with your books, choose your best one to unlock as a stretch later in the campaign. I have added extra illustrations to my books, unveiling them as stretch rewards even though I was already planning to include them. The same with under-jacket case art. There's an element of theater in planning out your stretches and revealing them to your backers.

You want to be careful, however. Don't hold back all the nice things that make your campaign attractive, or you might not get backers pledging in the first place.

The best stretch rewards are ones that don't cost you anything extra to create or ship but provide value to your backers. *All* your backers, both digital and physical. Good stretch rewards include bonus scenes or a new short story in your world, digital wallpapers and character art, a video call with your backers, a livestream of you doing a reading with a Q&A

afterward, backer names included in a special thank-you section of the book... The possibilities aren't endless, but there are certainly a lot of them. Be creative! I recorded a virtual Celtic fiddle concert for one reward.

Provide things that can upgrade all versions of the book, or be enjoyed in a digital version, like artwork or downloadable coloring pages. Or break up the rewards based on tiers. If I add a bookmark bonus, I'll provide printable digital files for my digital-only backers, and tuck a physical bookmark in with the print book (or send it in a letter-sized envelope if I'm drop-shipping the books).

Stretch reward ideas to get you started:

- Digital wallpapers (sized for phone and desktop)
- Character art (physical and digital)
- Backer names in a special Thank You section
- Maps
- Interior illustrations
- Coloring pages/bookmarks/postcards
- Custom chapter headers for digital and physical editions
- Bonus material—deleted scenes, new epilogue, bonus short story
- Bonus stickers/digital images
- Music playlist and author notes
- Author commentary audio
- Bookmarks—printable for digital backers, physical for print tiers
- Postcards

STRETCH GOALS

Stretch goals are a little different from stretch rewards, although people often use the terms interchangeably. In general, stretch goals are objectives to upgrade the book you are offering. They are *not necessarily* rewards that all backers will get. While some goals, like including a map, might benefit all backers, of both the digital and physical editions, other goals, like foiled dust jackets, only improve the hardcover edition of the book.

Special edition campaigns often set stretch goals for things like foiled covers, page edge designs, ribbon bookmarks, etc. While some of these upgrades might be included in the tier price, adding them to an offset print run inevitably increases the up-front cost to the author. Stretch goals add frills to the base product. Creators can set a funding goal low enough that they know their campaign will succeed without breaking the bank. Stretch goals are a way to provide extras while still making sure the project funds at a base level.

Authors sometimes create stretch goals for items that will be included in the top tiers, then offer those items as add-ons for the rest of their backers, for an additional cost. These can include transparent vellum overlays to go inside the book, extra swag, or even an audiobook version.

Be clear whether you're setting goals to upgrade your project, or unlocking rewards for all backers. There's a subtle difference. Both are useful strategies, but make sure you have a mix. You want every backer to feel like they're getting something extra as your campaign progresses.

SETTING UP YOUR STRETCHES

Whether you plan to offer stretch rewards, stretch goals, or a mix of both, it's important to be strategic about setting them up.

There's one very important guideline to follow: **Don't post the dollar amounts needed to unlock your stretch rewards in your campaign before you launch.**

Seriously. Do not put in the $ figures you aspire to hit in order to unlock the stretches. There is only one exception, and I'll discuss it in a minute.

Why shouldn't you post those dollar amounts? Because chances are good (and if this is your first campaign, *very* good) that you have miscalculated in one direction or the other. Either you have set the amounts too low and will blow through a bunch of your stretch rewards all at once, or you've set them too high and are in danger of not unlocking any of them.

Time after time, members of the Kickstarter for Authors Facebook Group say this is one of the most valuable pieces of advice they've gotten on their campaigns. They're right. No matter your hopes and fears, *you don't really know how your campaign will do until you launch.*

Setting your target amounts too low. If your campaign funds very quickly and continues to climb (it happens) you might end up unlocking a number of stretch rewards right away. This isn't ideal. If you've figured out five stretches over the course of your campaign, and you unlock three of them in the first two days, you'll be left scrambling to come up with more. You'll lose the opportunity to use them for promo later on in the campaign, or you might rush to add something that hurts your overall profitability.

While unlocking a bunch of your stretch rewards on the first day generally isn't a good idea, it can be a deliberate strategy. One author with a large fanbase launched her Kickstarter live in her Facebook group. She and her team planned to blast through about seven of the stretch rewards that first day, to keep the initial excitement high and build campaign momentum. It worked for her, but this is a strategy only a few authors will be able to use effectively.

Setting your target amounts too high. You don't want to set stretch rewards so high there's little chance of reaching them. If your campaign doesn't take off the way you were hoping, you'll lose the promo opportunities of announcing your stretch rewards and enticing new backers to pledge. It can be awkward if you set your stretch amount for $2k over your funding goal, but are only gaining $25 in pledges a day. If all your stretch reward amounts are out of reach, it's not appealing to backers.

The best strategy for stretches is to play your cards close to your chest. You want to reveal each new goal incrementally as your campaign progresses. Tell backers what your stretches will be, but don't reveal the amounts needed to unlock them. Instead, let backers know that the first goal will be announced after your campaign funds. Once you reach your funding goal and get a sense of your velocity, you can set your unlock goals for maximum impact. Keep in mind that your momentum will slow down after the first few days. It's fine to have the first stretch unlock at $1k above your funding goal, and then the second at a few hundred above that. Stretches don't have to unlock in even dollar increments.

I aim to reach a stretch reward every three to four days throughout my campaign. Once I unlock it, I set the amount to reach the next by looking at my campaign velocity. Sometimes I guess wrong, and must pivot, but that just keeps things exciting. Unlocking stretches gives me something fun to post about on social media and helps keep the pledge momentum going. I also like planning out those extra treats and goodies for my backers. Remember, a Kickstarter campaign is also an event!

When announcing you've reached your funding goals or unlocked stretches, remember the fluid nature of Kickstarter. Often, creators announce that a goal has been met, and then a cancelled pledge will drop them below that threshold. Play it safe. Wait until you're comfortably above the goal before broadcasting your victory.

A final reason to add extra rewards and upgrades to your campaign: to get fence-sitters off the fence.

Every project has people who follow the campaign without pledging. Many of them will not end up backing your project. The average conversion from follower to backer is between 10% and 30%.

If you continue to add upgrades and enticements throughout your campaign, you give those watchers more reason to jump in and become backers. They see the bonuses and decide it's worth it to make a pledge.

When not to use stretch rewards or goals.

If your campaign is moving very slowly toward your funding goal—so slowly that you might not fund until the very end of the campaign—then stretches will not be a useful strategy. You might be better off considering flash rewards, instead.

FLASH REWARDS

Flash rewards are time-limited goals that convey a sense of urgency and can help get a stalled campaign moving again. A flash reward can get new backers on board and also encourage your current backers to spread the word about your project.

These rewards often include smaller items like a downloadable coloring page, a new sticker design, or a backlist short story. Just like with your stretches, you want to make sure these are relatively low cost to produce.

When deciding to offer a flash reward, don't make your timeline too tight. Give yourself a few days to reach the goal. For example, if it's a Tuesday and your campaign is flagging, announce that the flash goal needs to be met by Friday at midnight to unlock the reward.

To figure out the goal for your flash reward, look at your campaign velocity. If you haven't had any pledges for several days, set a reasonable, small goal you think you could reach. While you could pin your flash reward to a dollar amount, I prefer setting it to a certain number of backers. Backer count is an easier metric to reach, as opposed to a funding amount, which can be a moving target. Five backers is five backers, but your funding from those backers could be anywhere from $5 to over $100.

Offer something easy to deliver that won't impact your bottom line. For one campaign, I offered an extra character card I was planning to include anyway, though backers got it early. For another, I used a bonus short story from my backlist. Both times, the flash reward worked to get my campaign moving again.

As with stretch rewards, don't forget to track these extra goodies and make sure you deliver them to your backers.

BACKER PERKS

Backer perks are rewards offered to all backers on a weekly basis simply for supporting the campaign. A new set of perks is unveiled each week. The idea behind these perks is to encourage backers to join your campaign early and stick around for the ongoing bonuses.

The rewards can be whatever you want, but remember your bottom line when offering bonus goodies to all backers. Digital rewards are going to be the best choice here, as they are low cost and easy to deliver. Authors with large backlists could offer a free digital book or short story per week. Sometimes, authors band together to offer digital collections of bonus books.

You can decide whether you want to deliver the perks during the campaign, or after it ends.

Deliver during the campaign. The advantage of delivering the weekly backer perks during the campaign is that it's generally easier. You can send a backer-only update at the end of each week with the link to download the bonus rewards. However, this also means that backers who end up cancelling their pledges later on will be able to scoop up the bonuses.

Deliver after the campaign ends. When you send the perks after the campaign ends, you know that only the people who backed your project and stayed for the duration are getting these rewards.

The disadvantage of waiting is that you'll need to keep track of when backers pledged, so you know who gets which weekly perks. Backers are numbered as they back. To track the dates, take note of what backer number you're on at those specific points in time. At week one, if fourteen people have pledged, then backers one to fourteen get the first-week perks. At week two, if you're up to twenty backers, everyone from one to twenty gets the week-two perks, etc.

When not to use stretches, goals, and perks.

If all these strategies seem like a lot of work, don't worry. They are optional. Once you get comfortable with using Kickstarter, you might want to use a few of these techniques to help you level up a future campaign and unlock bonuses for your fans. But none them are required. Plenty of successful campaigns do just fine without putting these more advanced strategies into play. Simple is a good approach, especially on a first campaign.

CHAPTER 8

YOUR STORY – THE HEART OF YOUR CAMPAIGN

- Essential Elements of Your Page
- Open with a Hook
- Expand Your Book Description
- Book Specs
- Entice with More
- Rewards
- Add-ons
- Stretch Rewards and Goals
- Why Kickstarter
- Shipping
- How Kickstarter Works
- What to Leave Out
- Risks
- Use of AI
- FAQ

The Story section of your Kickstarter campaign is where you let your project shine. It's a blank page—literally—waiting to be filled with hooky book descriptions, gorgeous graphics, a bit about yourself, and all the information a backer needs to enthusiastically support your project. Be yourself in this section. Let your unique voice and enthusiasm for your project come through. This isn't quite like writing marketing copy for a retailer. Kickstarter backers respond to a personal approach.

As you create your Story page, there are several big-picture things to keep in mind.

Think like a backer.

When building your page, keep your prospective backer firmly in mind. Make sure you're focusing on the things that are enticing and interesting to supporters. Inexperienced creators often make the mistake of focusing the campaign on what *they* want, not what prospective backers might like. Your job is to get people excited about what you're offering, and make it as irresistible as possible. Remember that "table at a convention" analogy? You're setting up your table, showing off your shiny books, and making your offerings appealing to people who wander by. Show them why it's worth their while to stop and check out your wares.

Use images and formatting.

Kickstarter is a very visual platform, so use lots of images! I recommend a graphic break every three to four paragraphs. It doesn't have to be a full image, although it can be. You can also use graphic headers to introduce your sections, snippets of art, the cover art, trope graphics featuring the cover, a book mockup, character sketches, maps, and images that convey the mood of your campaign.

When adding images to your campaign, Kickstarter give you the option to add captions. You can also add a description of the image for vision-impaired accessibility.

Use the formatting tools Kickstarter gives you in order to break up your walls of text. Bolds, italics, bullet lists, subheadings, and headings are your friends. You can now also embed media links hosted elsewhere, like YouTube and Spotify.

Build a clear Table of Contents.

Kickstarter has rolled out a new text editor that allows creators to generate a table of contents using the "heading" ability. Anything marked as a heading in the text editor will show up in a linked table of contents on the left side of the campaign. This helps backers easily navigate through your project, and is a great upgrade to the platform.

You can even use the heading ability for graphics. For example, if you've created a banner image with the word "Rewards" on a nice background, click your image and the text editor will open. Add the word "Rewards" as a heading, and that will show up in the table of contents.

Make sure not to use headings for emphasis. Subheadings are a better choice for anything you don't want to appear in the table of contents.

Remember mobile.

It's important to keep mobile devices in mind as you create your story. Are you using clear, uncluttered graphics? Breaking up big paragraphs of text? Many Kickstarter backers browse and pledge via their mobiles. In fact, some creators have reported over 40% of pledges coming from mobile devices. Preview your campaign on a mobile device to make sure your Story section isn't walls of text and cluttered, illegible images.

Avoid retailer terms.

Kickstarter won't approve campaigns that use retailer-like language. Don't use words like "preorder" or "presale." That language is useful when communicating to your readers off-platform, but not on Kickstarter. Try terms like "early release" instead.

Make it easy for people who haven't heard of your books to step into your world.

Kickstarter will show your campaign to many people who have no idea who you are. Make sure you're not leaving those prospective new readers out in the cold. Don't assume everyone who sees your campaign will know who you are or be familiar with your work. You will often get around 50% of your backers from Kickstarter (and up to 80% in some cases). Welcome new readers. Encourage them to pull up a chair, have a cup of tea, and hear about what you're offering.

Remember, too, that most of these potential backers aren't interested in dropping double digits on an unknown quantity. A $5 eBook series starter is essential, or another low-cost introduction to your world. Even if the focus of your campaign is on Book Two, make sure they can begin easily reading your series with an intro tier.

ESSENTIAL ELEMENTS OF YOUR STORY PAGE

Break your project up into several sections. Start with a hook to entice a prospective backer to read more. Describe a bit about your book. If you are offering a special edition, show it off! Explain your rewards, add-ons, and prospective stretch rewards. Introduce yourself. Have a brief section explaining why you're using Kickstarter to create your project. Explain how shipping will work for your campaign. Feel free to add anything else that you think backers should know or will help them get excited about your project. Kickstarter also requires you to fill out a Risks section and answer a couple questions about the use of AI in your project.

OPEN WITH A HOOK

Begin by telling backers about your book in an engaging and enticing way. Do not open with a monologue about your writing journey (unless that's what your book is about), your bio, the finances, or even all the bells and whistles of the special edition. You need to interest backers in your book, first and foremost. (Granted, this might not matter as much to some collectors, but most Kickstarter backers are readers and want to care about your story.)

Some authors find the "three questions" format works for them. "Do you love X? Think Y is awesome? Want more Z? Then check out this project!" If you have a great tagline or hooky elevator pitch, this is the place to put it. Comparisons to other books or media can be used here. Just make sure that your book really *is* like *Star Wars* with talking horses set on Middle Earth.

In some genres (generally romance-related), a trope graphic can be very effective. This is an image of your book surrounded by keywords and tropes. *Kickass heroine. Rivals to lovers. Epic space battles. Dragons!* Squiggly lines with arrows connect each trope/element to the book, making it crystal-clear what backers can expect to find inside. If you choose to use a trope graphic, make sure the words are in high contrast to the background, and that it's easy to read on mobile.

If you don't use a trope graphic, follow your book hook with a strong visual image that communicates a sense of the book/world/characters.

EXPAND YOUR BOOK DESCRIPTION

Put a heading next, either in text or a heading-tagged banner, that says something like "About (the Book title/series)."

Introduce your world, the stakes, and your characters in an engaging way. This is also the place to emphasize what makes your work special and unique. What made you excited about writing this book? Add images to help bring your descriptions to life. Don't forget to break up blocks of paragraphs with graphics.

In this section, include a link to where prospective backers can read a sample of your work. You can send them to a BookFunnel sample, or even a page on your website where you've posted the first few chapters.

If you have a couple reviews of your book, include them here. I recommend no more than two short and glowing ones. If your campaign is for a series with multiple books, you can say a little bit about each title, accompanied by a single review for that book. Don't forget to show off the book covers and character artwork.

ADD YOUR BOOK SPECS

Again, lead with a heading that tells backers what's next. Then show off the physical edition of what you'll be creating. 3D book mockup images are vital here, especially if you're making a special edition. I recommend a bullet list with the following:

- Genre
- Format
- Trim size
- Page count
- Signed (if you're autographing)

Continue with any of the following your book might include:

- Bonus material
- Spice level
- Content warning
- Number of included books, if it's an omnibus
- Unique chapter graphics
- Custom two-page chapter headers
- Illustrations (black and white, or color)
- Duplex cover (for paperbacks)
- Special case art under the dust jacket
- Foiled case design
- Sprayed edges
- Endpapers
- Numbered editions
- Faux-leather cover
- Ribbon bookmark

You get the idea. It's important to highlight all the elements so that backers can see at a glance what they're pledging for.

If you're including custom formatting or illustrations, create some eye-catching interior mockup graphics to show off those elements. For deluxe special editions, linger over each special thing. If your spines make an extra design when lined up, devote a separate image and description to that. Don't make a big graphic and toss all the elements in. Remember, you're selling a luxury edition. Inhale the rich paper scent. Feel the suppleness of the binding. Admire the glittering foiled insets on the faux-leather cover...

Some authors prefer to put the special edition features above the expanded story description, so prospective backers will get that information first. Lay out your campaign however feels best to you. But if you launch and aren't seeing the hoped-for results, try switching things around during the campaign.

MORE ABOUT WHAT YOU'RE OFFERING

After your book specs, you can add a section with more information about your project. Expand on what you're offering, either by going into more detail about your book, your characters, talking about artwork, narrators, or anything special about how this story came to be. Just remember to keep in interesting and engaging. Prospective backers don't need to hear about every little step of your process.

REWARDS

Although you created reward tiers that backers can check out, it's also a good idea to describe your rewards here. You can use bigger and better images than in the reward tiers, and the text is much more legible. If you have multi-part rewards like swag packs, this is a good opportunity to show those items off.

Some creators separate the tiers into two "tracks." First, they describe the digital offerings by tier, then the physical ones. That way, backers can see everything that's available in their preferred formats.

ADD-ONS

This is where you entice people to add your extras to their reward pledge. Let prospective backers know what else you have to offer, but don't make this section longer than the rewards section. Use images and strong, snappy descriptions.

STRETCH REWARDS AND GOALS

Let backers know what you are planning to add once your funding goal is met. Have fun and treat your readers! Just remember not to include the dollar amounts needed to unlock the stretches before your campaign is live. You won't have a good idea of how your funding velocity is going until after you launch, and you don't want to mess up by setting the amounts too low, or too high.

WHY KICKSTARTER

Creators often add a bit about why they have chosen to bring their project to Kickstarter. This adds a personal touch, and lets backers know you're not just thinking of Kickstarter like another retailer platform, or supporters like anonymous buyers. Talk about what special thing you can provide your fans by using Kickstarter as opposed to simply releasing your book on retailers. Remember to keep the *crowd* in crowdfunding.

ABOUT THE AUTHOR

Don't forget to add a bit about yourself! Make sure it's in first person. Backers like to know who they are supporting on Kickstarter. Let them get to know you a little. Include a photo if you want.

SHIPPING

It's a good idea to explain how your shipping is going to work. Whether you are including U.S. shipping in your reward tiers, having Kickstarter add on the shipping after a backer pledges, or charging after your campaign ends with a third-party pledge manager, you need to let backers know what to expect.

Add a disclaimer here about not being responsible for international VAT or extra import fees a backer might need to pay to receive their overseas package.

Mention if you are willing to add shipping to individual countries upon request. If you plan to drop-ship books internationally and send any swag and signed bookplates separately, let backers know.

HOW KICKSTARTER WORKS

If you anticipate bringing a bunch of new people to Kickstarter, consider adding a brief description of how the platform works. Let backers know that their credit cards won't be charged until the campaign ends. If you plan on any stretch rewards or goals, mention that the project will continue to add bonuses and that you'll be sending updates along the way.

WHAT TO LEAVE OUT OF YOUR STORY SECTION

There are some things you don't need to include on your project page. Going in-depth on the finances isn't recommended unless you have a very high funding goal or your rewards are more expensive than is usual on Kickstarter. You also want to keep an engaging tone throughout. Bitter diatribes or poor-me stories will generally turn backers away.

Kickstarter allows you to create a pie chart breaking down your funding. This is very common in games, tech projects, and other categories where a large funding goal is the norm. Backers want to know where that $200k funding raise is going.

Books are different. Campaigns with low funding goals making POD books don't need to include a detailed funding breakdown. Most book campaigns don't use the funding pie chart.

Along with leaving out the nitty-gritty funding details, don't spend a lot of time talking about how expensive it is to self-publish. People understand that authors need money. It's why we're on Kickstarter, after all. But it's always better to focus on what the backer gets out of supporting our projects, not how much we need their cash.

Finally, try to keep personal negativity out of your campaign. You don't have to be all sweetness and light, but you also don't want to turn prospective supporters away.

Once you complete your Story, there are two more required sections for you to fill out: Risks, and Use of AI.

RISKS

There are always risks of some kind. Paper shortages, shipping delays, vendors unable to provide what you need, unexpected emergencies, health issues—all of those things can impact your campaign. In addition to mentioning the potential risks, reassure backers. If you're an experienced self-publisher who has created print copies of your books before, let them know. If you have successfully run and fulfilled Kickstarter campaigns in the past, say so.

USE OF AI

Kickstarter wants you to disclose the use of AI in your project. First, they ask whether your campaign is going to develop AI technology, which will not apply to most authors. Second, they ask whether you're using AI-generated content in your project or campaign. They don't give a lot of instruction, just a text box for you to explain how you are using AI. Some creators use generative AI art engines like Midjourney to create images for their campaign and for their books. Others find that the various AI writing tools are helpful in their process.

Kickstarter's aim is transparency. They are not making judgments about your campaign. They just want disclosure because some backers want to know.

If you are using generative AI in your project, it's best to disclose. Answer yes, then fill out the questions accordingly. When Kickstarter asks if you have consent to use your AI-generated content, most creators are answering yes, that they have the appropriate commercial licenses from the programs used to make the content.

FAQ

You have one more optional section you can add: the FAQ. This is the place to explain anything potentially confusing or different about your campaign, or expand a bit in anticipation of backer questions.

The FAQ is set up in a question-and-answer format. You can add to this section before or after your campaign launches. It's a great place to address backer questions when your campaign is live.

CHAPTER 9
PEOPLE

- People
- Your Profile and Pen Name
- Vanity URL

PEOPLE

The next section is where you fill out your creator bio, including a photo if you want, and links to your website and Facebook. Your profile displays publicly.

YOUR PROFILE AND PEN NAME

You can put any name in your creator bio: your pen name, your publishing house, etc. However, *Kickstarter also displays your legal name on your profile*, which is drawn from the banking information you fill out in the Payment section.

If you need to keep your real name private (as many authors do), you will need to contact Kickstarter to have them show your pen name instead. Here's what to do, according to Kickstarter. "Kickstarter creators are required to use their legal names for the sake of transparency (more at kickstarter.com/privacy). Authors who write under pen names and are looking to protect their legal names can reach out to our support team via our help center: https://help.kickstarter.com/hc/en-us/requests/new. Select 'name change' as the ticket subject to ensure it gets routed to the appropriate team. We cannot promise all requests will be granted as exceptions to our policies are only made under certain circumstances."

Be aware that you'll need to go through the above steps to change your name with every new campaign you set up on the platform.

Next, you can add an image, which can be a photo or an avatar.

For the bio section, keep it brief. Kickstarter recommends three hundred characters or less.

There's a privacy box, but if you check it, people won't be able to see your biography, websites, or any campaigns you have supported. It does not hide your name or legal name. For creators using Kickstarter, it's probably best to leave your information public so that people can find out more about you.

Add your location next. This is required. It can be a big city near you if you don't feel comfortable putting your town. The time zone adjusts automatically based on your location, so you don't need to add it in the next box.

VANITY URL

Other than your name and bio, your Vanity URL is the most important item on this page. This is the URL that will show before the title of any campaign you make on Kickstarter. For example, "kickstarter.com/Fiddleheadpress/campaign-name." It should be your pen name or publishing company. **Do not make this the name of your campaign!** Once you fill it in and get approval on your first campaign, it cannot be changed for subsequent projects.

The final thing you can do on this page is add your websites and Facebook page. These will be hyperlinked in your creator profile.

Collaborator(s)

You can add a collaborator to your project. Collaborators can edit your project, communicate with backers, and help coordinate reward fulfillment. If you have multiple creators working on a project, or want to give your assistant access, add their Kickstarter account names here. There are a few companies that help authors run their campaigns. This kind of help and collaboration can be invaluable, especially with campaigns that have a high funding goals and could reach hundreds or thousands of backers.

Collaborators can have their own campaigns running simultaneously.

Demographics

This is an optional survey that asks a number of questions about you and your campaign. Kickstarter uses the information they gather here to help them "support a diverse and equitable creator community."

CHAPTER 10
PAYMENT PAGE

There are five essential sections on this page: your contact info, whether you're an individual or business running the campaign, verification of your tax information, your banking details, and a payment method you must provide to Kickstarter.

The first two, your email and the project type, are fairly self-explanatory. Most authors will be running campaigns as an individual. Unless you are fully incorporated, that is probably your best choice. If you have questions about this, reach out to Kickstarter support for additional clarity.

Project Verification

This is where you prove that you're a real person, and provide your tax details. This is done through the third-party application, Stripe. This section can get glitchy! Make sure you save often. If you correctly filled out your Stripe details and the page isn't letting you move forward to your banking details, try saving and then refreshing the page.

Banking Details

Provide your bank account details so that Kickstarter can deposit your money via electronic funds transfer. Again, if this section glitches, try saving and/or refreshing.

Payment

The final thing to fill out on this page is your credit or debit card details. Kickstarter needs a way to charge you if you end up providing refunds to backers or in the unlikely event of chargebacks.

CHAPTER 11
PROJECT REVIEW

You did it! Every section of your campaign has been filled out. That's a huge milestone.

Submit for Kickstarter approval

Your next step is to submit your campaign for Kickstarter approval. It's recommended to do this as early in the process as possible. Even if you don't feel "done" with your campaign, it's important to get a prelaunch page up so you can start gathering followers for your campaign. You can only set up a prelaunch page once your project has been approved.

Approval, especially for a first-time campaign, can take one to three days. If the platform is particularly busy, it can take up to a week for your project to be approved.

Don't spend too much time perfecting your project page before putting it in for approval. You simply need to have something in each of the basic sections. At least one reward, the start of a strong story, the risks section and financials completed, etc. Kickstarter isn't judging how good your campaign looks. They just want to make sure you're not breaking any of their rules.

You can continue to edit your campaign after it's approved, refining, tweaking, and building it out in all its glory.

Beware the green button

As soon as your campaign is approved, you have the option to launch it immediately. Do not touch that button until the moment you want to make your campaign live. Don't accidentally hit it early. The moment you click it and answer "yes," your project will be live on Kickstarter.

Setting up your prelaunch page

You'll do this in the Promotion tab, which is covered in the next section.

While it's possible to go directly from approval to live, your campaign has a better chance of success if you give it some time in prelaunch. Spread the word to your readers and gather followers. When you **do** launch, you'll have people ready to pledge immediately and help give your project visibility on the Kickstarter platform.

CHAPTER 12
PROMOTION PAGE

You can't do anything on the promotion page until after your campaign is approved. Once it is, you'll want to make use of the various tools Kickstarter gives you to track your promotional efforts.

Project URL

Kickstarter will generate your project page URL from the title of your campaign. Once it does, this name cannot be changed. If your campaign title is something like "Faerie Hearts: A Romantic Fantasy Collection," that entire thing will become your campaign URL.

To keep your URL streamlined, go to your Basics tab and temporarily change the title of your project to something shorter. Make sure to copy and save the title you worked so hard on, so that you can restore it once you're done setting the project URL. For example, I shortened the above title to "Faerie Hearts," saved that title in the Basics, then returned to the Promotions page to generate the project URL.

Once your URL is generated, go back into the Basics tab and restore your original project title.

Prelaunch Page

The prelaunch page displays your banner, title, and subtitle, plus your location and your project categories. There's a button that interested people can click to be notified when your campaign launches. Nobody can see your rewards or the main body of your project via the prelaunch page. If you are setting up a very early prelaunch, months before your book cover art is ready, you can use a placeholder image on your banner. Just make sure you replace it with the final artwork by the time your campaign launches.

Click on the "Activate my page" button, and you'll be taken to a preview of what your prelaunch page will look like. You'll need to confirm on the upper right to finish creating the prelaunch page.

The URL of your prelaunch page will also be the URL of your campaign once it goes live.

Custom Referral Tags

Kickstarter allows creators to make up to five hundred unique trackable links. Use them! These let you see where your backers came from and which of your promotional efforts are working the best.

Create a custom referral tag to share in your newsletter, one for your Facebook page, one for cross-promotional efforts, one for your website. Basically, anywhere you'll be sharing a link to your project. You can use these links while in prelaunch as well as when your campaign is live. Give each link a name that will help you identify where it came from: myFB, nl, swaps, etc.

Be aware that these custom links will not give you any tracking information until your campaign is live. They will give data after your campaign launches and a backer pledges. The links only track pledges, not clicks.

However, the Kickstarter platform currently cannot track back through multiple links to see where your backer originated from. For example, you can share the prelaunch page via a tracking link to your social media to gain followers. But Kickstarter sends an email to all followers when your campaign launches. It's unclear whether they take credit for the backers who pledge via that email link, even though you brought the backer to Kickstarter in the first place via your social media.

Kickstarter provides a lot of data to creators about where backers are coming from. In addition to your personal tracking links, they will identify whether a backer arrived via Facebook or another outside source on the web, or came via one of the many places your campaign might have been shown on the Kickstarter platform.

Google Analytics, Meta Pixel, and Meta Conversions API Access Token

These tracking and conversion tools can help you see where your backers are coming from and how they are converting from your social media and other web applications. They are powerful when used well. A crash course on harnessing their power is outside the scope of this book. Check the Resources for more.

What's next?

Your Promotion page is set up and your campaign is in prelaunch. Congrats! The next section will give you some promo strategies and techniques to help get your readers excited about your upcoming project.

PART THREE
CAMPAIGN STAGES FROM PRELAUNCH TO FULFILLMENT

CHAPTER 13
PRELAUNCH

- How Long Should Your Prelaunch Last?
- Fabulous Followers
- Warming Up Your Fans
- Should You Advertise?
- Sharing the Preview
- When to Go Live

Prelaunch is the period of time between when your campaign is approved by Kickstarter and when you make it live.

HOW LONG SHOULD YOUR PRELAUNCH LAST?

While it's possible to launch your project as soon as Kickstarter approves it, I don't recommend you do. Best practice is to have a prelaunch page up for at least two weeks before you make your campaign live. This gives you time to gather prospective backers to follow your project. As soon as you launch your campaign, those followers will receive an email from Kickstarter. Having some strong early support for your project can give it a solid launch and help get you to your funding goal in a matter of days, or even hours.

Some creators have their campaigns in prelaunch for up to a year. Others prefer the bare minimum. I tend to shoot for a month or two, ideally launching my campaigns with at least fifty followers.

FABULOUS FOLLOWERS

Followers are the people who have clicked the "notify me on launch" button on your preview page before your campaign goes live. You will also continue to gain followers after you launch and during the duration of your campaign. Those people click the "Remind me" button under the pledge button on your project page. Once you launch, followers are those who are watching, but have not yet backed, your campaign.

How many followers should you have before launch?

Currently, I recommend you try to gather a minimum of twenty-five followers before launching your campaign. If you have a higher funding goal, try for at least one hundred prelaunch followers. When if comes to prelaunch followers, more is always better. You can see the number of followers on your dashboard in the Promotions section. Once you have ten people following, the number will also publicly display on your prelaunch page.

Outside the book ecosystem, a much higher number of followers is recommended before a creator launches their campaign. This is because those campaigns tend to have higher stakes, and higher funding goals. Some of those projects spend months advertising and building a mailing list specifically for their Kickstarter campaign before they launch.

Authors have it easier. Many of us already have mailing lists and social media presences. However, it's important to warm up your audience to the idea of Kickstarter before you launch.

Finding followers

As soon as your prelaunch page is up, start spreading the world about your project. Promote your upcoming Kickstarter campaign to your fans and readers. Post about it on your social media and to your newsletter. Don't forget to use your tracking links, as mentioned earlier.

Let people know why they should support your project on Kickstarter! Talk about the extra or exclusive things they can only get by backing your project. This can include bonus swag, getting the book early, or a special edition that won't be offered on retailers.

Make sure your readers know their support makes a big difference on Kickstarter as opposed to just buying your books on the big retailer platforms. Your fans get to be angel investors and receive awesome rewards in return.

If you are offering early-bird rewards, let your fans know well in advance. People will want to back your campaign in the first day or two so they don't miss out. Make sure they know the best way to do that is by following your project.

There are other creative ways to get readers to your prelaunch page. Some authors plan cover reveals on their prelaunch banner. Others provide rewards to their readers for helping spread the word. The key thing is to bring your readers over to Kickstarter, so they can help you with a strong launch.

Introduce your readers to the idea of Kickstarter early on. It's a good idea to spotlight campaigns from other creators that your fans might enjoy (and are similar to what you're planning to offer). Explain how Kickstarter helps authors create awesome editions of their books, and how backers get rewards when they pledge. Share the simple steps of how to pledge to a campaign.

The more you can do in advance to demystify the platform and get your readers excited about your campaign, the better.

Follower to backer conversion

Once you launch, some of the people following your campaign will convert to backers by making a pledge. You will also continue to gain followers—alternatively called "watchers" on some parts of your project dashboard.

Do not expect the majority of followers to turn into backers. People follow campaigns for various reasons. Some might intend to pledge, but are unable to for financial reasons. Some might be watching to see what stretch rewards or bonus goodies are unlocked by the end. Some might be other creators curious to see how your campaign does.

Successful campaigns can see anywhere from 10% to 80% conversion. (I've only ever heard of one campaign reaching that high, however—the next one down was 65%.) Most campaigns will be between 15% and 30%. Don't take it personally when only a small number of followers turn into backers. That doesn't mean your campaign has failed. It's just how Kickstarter works.

WARMING UP YOUR FANS

Authors are often surprised to find that very few people from their mailing lists and social media back their campaign. There are a few reasons that people are resistant to supporting a campaign on Kickstarter. Your job is to help them get past that resistance and excited about pledging to your campaign.

Many people still think Kickstarter is like GoFundMe. Make the differences clear by explaining how Kickstarter is helping you produce a new book or special edition. Encourage your fans to support you directly by pledging to your campaign, and don't be shy about telling them what they get out of it. An early copy of the book, special bonuses and goodies, etc. Reassure them their credit cards won't be charged until after your campaign ends successfully.

Like any new website, there is a barrier to entry for people unfamiliar with the platform. They have to learn a new system. They have to make yet another account and put in their credit card details. You'll need to overcome those objections by making it clear why using Kickstarter is a great thing for them, as well as for you.

Help your readers get used to the idea of Kickstarter by spotlighting other creators' campaigns in your newsletter or social media. Highlight the ones you've supported. Talk about why you pledged and what exciting rewards you're looking forward to getting.

SHOULD YOU ADVERTISE?

If your Facebook ad game is strong, you might have some success running ads to your Kickstarter campaign. However, it's difficult to gauge the success of your ads until your project is live and you can see which tracking links lead to pledges.

Do NOT respond to any of the emails you'll start getting from people promising to help you find backers. They cannot help you. There are a few legitimate companies that can successfully find backers for other types of projects, like games or comics. But they cannot help you find book backers. This is because the Publishing ecosystem on Kickstarter is still developing. There isn't yet a strongly established base of hundreds of thousands of book campaign backers that can be reliably advertised to.

If you're considering hiring a reputable company to help you advertise, ask them what book campaigns, *specifically*, they have run advertising for. Then reach out to those authors and ask about their experience with the company.

In general, the only reason to hire an advertising company is if you anticipate having a campaign that will break six figures. Even then, their efforts might not be able to move the needle all that much. This will change once the books side of Kickstarter starts to become as robust as games, comics, and tech.

Some creators have had success hiring BackerKit Launch to help with emailing supporters. This is generally more effective once you've run one or more campaigns and have previous backers their system can reach out to.

If you are making a deluxe special edition, some of the book tour companies now offer a Kickstarter option. They can help share your campaign via influencers on platforms like Instagram and TikTok. If your genre does well on those platforms, you might consider one of those companies.

SHARING THE PREVIEW

Your campaign preview is not the same as the prelaunch page. The preview is the behind-the-scenes look at your project page and rewards. Share your preview link with others so they can look at your campaign and provide feedback before it launches.

Your project doesn't need to be approved, or even in prelaunch, for you to share your preview. To generate a preview link, do the following:

- Go to your project and click on Preview on the upper left (look for the green eye-shaped icon).
- From there, click on "manage sharing."
- A pop-up will open. Copy that link. That's the link to share the behind-the-scenes look at your project.

Some creators share the campaign preview link with their readers to generate interest and excitement. Invite your fans to give feedback on the campaign. This will get them engaged and help you give them the rewards they want.

I recommend you share the preview link with other creators to get valuable feedback before you launch. Ask your friends to take a look and let you know if there's anything unclear or confusing. Even better, join the Kickstarter for Authors group, where you can post your preview link and get invaluable advice from experienced creators about what's working in your campaign and what needs tweaking.

You can also hire me for a Campaign Prelaunch Flight Check, if you'd like expert eyes on your project before you launch. There's a link in the resources.

WHEN TO GO LIVE

At some point, you'll need to make your project live, no matter how many followers you have or how much time you've spent polishing up your campaign. There's no way to ensure a perfect launch. Do what you can, but don't let any of the above stop you from doing the most important thing…

Launching your campaign.

CHAPTER 14
LAUNCH!

- Ingredients for a Successful Launch
- Big Green Button Time
- Spread the Word
- Immediate Spam
- Celebrate!
- Funding Velocity and Campaign Trajectory

Launching your campaign can be nerve-racking. After all your preparation and hard work, it's the moment of truth. *Is this going to work?*

There's only one way to find out. But if you've done all of the following, your project will be set up for success.

INGREDIENTS FOR A SUCCESSFUL LAUNCH

- You have a project you feel passionate about and are excited to share.

- You have followers ready to support your campaign right away.
- It's early in the week (Monday or Tuesday).
- It's early in the day (U.S. time zones).
- You've gotten feedback to help polish your campaign.
- Your project opens with a hook and has strong graphics.
- You've crafted a compelling and interesting story page.
- You've priced your reward tiers attractively.
- You have set a reasonable funding goal.

BIG GREEN BUTTON TIME

After carefully avoiding the green button until now, it's finally time to click it! From your dashboard, select your project name on the upper left. Then click the green "I'm ready to launch" button.

That's it! Your campaign is now live on Kickstarter.

Once your project is live, try not to hold your breath for the first hour. Go make a cup of tea. Maybe it's a good morning for a walk.

If you launched live with your fans, celebrate, hand out door prizes, and share the excitement.

If you'd rather pull the blankets over your head and not look for a few hours, that's fine too.

Ideally, your numbers are starting to tick up and you're headed toward your funding goal. So, what's next?

SPREAD THE WORD

Kickstarter will notify all the people who followed your campaign the moment it goes live. That should give you some initial pledges. Go on your social media and let people know your campaign is live. If you have early-bird rewards, talk them up. Send out a newsletter later in the day, reminding your subscribers that your exciting new project is now live on Kickstarter.

SPAM-STORM

One of the unfortunate side effects of running a Kickstarter is the number of scam promoters who will immediately contact you. None of them can help you. Report as spam (there's a button for that above the message on your Kickstarter dashboard). If they track you to your website, your Facebook, your other platforms, ignore and delete. After a while they will go away. Do not engage with any of them. And please, do not hire them. Resist the urge to set your money on fire.

As mentioned previously, there are a few legitimate promotion companies who help advertise Kickstarter campaigns. They currently can't do much for a book project, and it's unlikely they are spamming your inbox for business.

CELEBRATE!

Don't forget the fun aspects of running a campaign. Share the excitement with your fans and backers, especially if the pledges are flying in and you hit your funding goal on day one.

STAY GROUNDED IN REALITY

Your funding velocity will slow down after a few days.

If your pledges skyrocketed in the first few hours, don't assume you'll end up with an amazing final dollar amount. Unfortunately, that launch momentum will not sustain.

Every campaign slows down. Even Brandon Sanderson had slow-ish days. Keep in mind that a lot of campaigns raise one-third of their funding in the first few days. The second third is spread out throughout the middle of the campaign. The last third comes in during the final few days.

That said, every campaign is unique.

Not all campaigns follow the quick rise, slow middle, end uptick pattern. Some are slow and steady all the way. Some struggle to hit their funding goal, with plenty of frustrating ups and downs.

Whatever trajectory your campaign takes, try not to compare it with other projects on the platform. Comparison is the thief of joy. Celebrate your wins, large and small.

CHAPTER 15
YOUR PROJECT IS LIVE

- Your Campaign Page
- Project Page Dashboard
- Backer Communication
- What You Can Change
- What if You're Getting no Pledges?
- Reaching the Funding Goal
- Project We Love

Once you've launched, it can be tempting to spend a lot of time staring at your project dashboard. However, unless you are getting no pledges at all, try not to worry about how your funding is going.

Now that your campaign is live, there are two new areas to explore on your project page. The first is on your live campaign page, where there is a row of options underneath your banner image. These are: Campaign, Rewards, FAQ, Updates, Comments, and Community. These are part of your public-facing project page, and anyone can click on them. The second is your project dashboard menu on the left side of your page, which only you can see.

YOUR CAMPAIGN PAGE

Campaign

This takes you to the project home page on Kickstarter.

Rewards

This opens up your rewards in a new page that's different from how the rewards are displayed on your project page. This is a newer interface that Kickstarter recently rolled out along with the ability for creators to add images to their items. It's a nice way to see the reward tier images and the individual item images at a slightly larger size. It's also easier for backers to click between the rewards and compare them.

FAQ

If you created some questions and answers in the FAQ section when creating your campaign, those show up here.

Updates

All updates you create will post here. Backers will also be emailed every time you make an update. Prospective backers can read your updates here to see project news and how you are communicating it. You have the option of making backer-only updates, but that's only recommended when you're giving campaign-sensitive information like links to all-backer rewards. Sending regular updates is an important part of your campaign. We'll talk more about that shortly.

Comments

Backers can leave comments on your project page and on updates. It's surprisingly easy to miss seeing these, even if you have notifications turned on. Check the comments and updates regularly. Often, backers leave questions about your campaign as comments on the project. Make sure to answer them publicly. Kickstarter likes to see transparent interaction between the creator and backers. Backers sometimes leave general messages of support, too, which is always nice.

Community

This is a page with some simple metrics. It tells what cities and countries your backers are coming from, and how many are new to Kickstarter. If you are bringing some new supporters to the platform, pat yourself on the back.

YOUR PROJECT PAGE DASHBOARD MENU

From your project page, you now have a new menu of options on the left-hand side. There are three main sections: Project, Campaign, and Pledge Management.

Project

In the project section you can view the campaign as it appears to backers on Kickstarter, without the creator option menu on the left. You can also edit your project. Clicking "Edit" will take you to the familiar editing page with basics, rewards, etc. The final thing you can do in this section is add collaborators and give them permission to edit the campaign and interact with backers. If your project has a team, you'll have good reason to use this.

Campaign

The campaign section is where you'll find all your lovely data and analytics.

Advanced Analytics

Click this link and you'll discover an almost overwhelming amount of information. The things I find most useful here are the metrics about former backers and how many pledges are coming via mobile. If you're a data nerd, you'll be in heaven. Be aware that these analytics are in beta, and the link will disappear once your campaign ends.

Dashboard

This is your campaign's main HQ. Front and center is your campaign funding, number of backers, and a graph charting your progress. In addition to the funding progress, you can see where backers are coming from (via referral links, Kickstarter, or other web locations). You can keep an eye on your follower-to-backer conversion, plus see which reward tiers are getting the most pledges. The bottom of the page shows individual backer pledges, upgrades, and cancellations. It also tracks when you send out backer updates.

One of the things that astonishes new creators is the amount of data Kickstarter gives on the campaign dashboard. We can see where backers are coming from, whether they are super-active on the platform or brand new, what the average pledge amount is across all tiers, how many pledges you have for each tier, and much more. Spending some time with those metrics can help you refine your campaign and give you insight into setting up your next one for even more success.

Messages

The message section here is different from the messages you see when you click on your profile link. Communications here are specific to your campaign. Be aware that messages sent here, for reasons unknown, don't always show up in your notifications. Make a note to check regularly and respond to new messages from backers and prospective backers.

Unfortunately, as already mentioned, random spammers will message you, trying to get you to buy their services. I mark them as spam, and never respond.

Updates

Updating backers is an important part of running your campaign. Backers receive an email from Kickstarter when you create an update. The update also appears on the updates tab below the banner image on your project page. Most of the time, you'll want to make your updates public, unless you are sharing information you only want backers to see, like a link to a special reward.

Use updates to let your supporters know when you hit important milestones like funding or stretch goals. Send an update when you have any other worthy news about the campaign, like adding new tiers or add-ons or opening shipping to more countries.

When you make an update, Kickstarter emails it to everyone who has already backed. Backers won't necessarily circle back around and keep rereading your project page, so keep them in the loop by using updates.

How often to send updates

I recommend you send an update every three to four days to keep your backers in the loop and connected with your campaign. Once your campaign ends, use updates regularly to let backers know how fulfillment is going.

Editing and glitches

There are a couple of known glitches when creating an update in the text editor. The first is that your images might fail to load.

To fix the failed image upload, save your update. Then refresh the page, and try again. The Kickstarter system tends to time out if you've been working for a while on a page. Both here and elsewhere on the platform it's always a good idea to save often, and refresh the page if you start having issues.

Although you can edit the update as it appears on the project page for thirty minutes after sending it, the auto-email that went out to backers cannot be changed. Because of this, I recommend you always preview your update before sending it.

Pledge Management

The Backer Report is a key part of your dashboard. You'll be using it throughout your campaign, both while live and during fulfillment. It is a data table containing backer information and links to individual pledge records. You can sort your backers by tier and add-ons, which is useful when it comes time to fulfill your rewards.

Remember, Kickstarter requires that you not share backer information. It is only for fulfilling your project rewards.

On the Backer Report page there is an option to message all backers. In general, use it sparingly. Kickstarter is big on transparency and prefers that creators use the public-facing updates when communicating with backers.

You can see individual backer information by clicking the backer's name in the backer report table. From there, you can send them an individual message, or leave a note to yourself about their pledge.

Backer Survey

Once your campaign ends, you'll have the ability to send out **one** backer survey per pledge tier. The fulfillment section will also open up, giving you helpful tools and information. We'll go over the backer survey in the fulfillment section of this book.

Post update

The big "Post update" button opens up the section to create an update for your backers.

Finally, there's a creator resource section at the very bottom of the left-hand menu. Some of the links are a few years out of date, while others lead to useful information. I recommend the Creator Handbook and FAQ. If you need to open a help ticket for your campaign, click on "Support."

BACKER COMMUNICATION

The people who choose to support your campaign are pure gold. Treat them well. Communicate frequently via updates. Keep an eye on the comments and respond to each one. Reach out individually when appropriate. Stay responsive and open.

I've seen a number of creators use Google surveys (sent via updates) to poll their backers about preferred next stretch rewards or new add-ons as the campaign progresses. This keeps backers engaged and gives them a voice in the ongoing project.

Thanking backers

Some creators send their backers a thank-you message after they pledge. I send individual thank-yous to new backers every evening, letting them know I appreciate their support. Some pledge managers, like BackerKit, might also provide this as an auto-response option once a backer pledges.

WHAT YOU CAN (AND CAN'T) CHANGE

Remember that your project isn't a static thing. You'll want to keep making changes to your campaign while you're live.

The following *can* be edited while the project is live:

- Project category
- Project title and description
- Project video and image
- New rewards, including add-ons, or rewards without backers.
- Rewards quantity (this can be increased but not decreased)
- Image on a reward tier or add-on
- Project FAQs
- Kickstarter profile bio

The following *cannot* be edited after the project has launched:

- Funding goal
- Project deadline
- Reward tiers and add-ons that have already been selected by a backer (only the image can be edited)
- Information in the Payment tab, including your bank account and verified identity.
- Kickstarter profile name

WHAT IF YOU'RE GETTING NO PLEDGES?

If you've launched and are getting no support for your project, take a good look at your title, subtitle, and banner. Make sure they're doing their job to pull prospective backers in. If they are solid, and your campaign is clear and enticing, then it's time to get out there and connect with your readers and fans. Talk up your campaign on social media. Send a newsletter to your mailing list. Let people know why they should support your awesome book project on Kickstarter.

REACHING THE FUNDING GOAL

The first big campaign milestone is reaching is your funding goal. This could happen within the first day, or take most of the campaign to achieve.

When you reach your goal, get ready to celebrate with your backers. Just make sure to wait until you have a few more pledges come in, so there's extra padding before you make your announcement. It can be disheartening to reach your funding the goal, and then have a dropped pledge put you back under it again.

One you are a few pledges over your goal, make a backer update. Celebrate reaching your goal, and let backers know what's next for the campaign. Are you planning on rolling out stretch goals or rewards? Figure out your target for reaching the first one and let your backers know.

PROJECT WE LOVE

Kickstarter staff hand-select a small number of projects for Project We Love status. If your campaign is selected, it will get a bit more visibility on the platform. Plus, Kickstarter sends you a cool badge to use in your social media.

Project We Love exists to bring notice to projects that are different and exceptional, and to showcase the best the platform has to offer. When building your campaign, bring your unique self to the page. What makes your project different and wonderful?

Here's an article from Kickstarter on how to get featured as a Project We Love. https://www.kickstarter.com/blog/how-to-get-featured-on-kickstarter

Keep in mind that plenty of successful projects aren't selected. Don't worry if your campaign isn't chosen. It doesn't mean you won't succeed.

CHAPTER 16
THE SAGGY MIDDLE

- Supercharge Your Socials
- Tweak Your Campaign
- Try a Flash Reward
- Use the Kickstarter Platform
- Cross-promote with Other Creators
- Cancelled Pledges
- Maintain Your Sanity
- When to Consider Cancelling Your Campaign

It's common for a campaign to have a solid amount of pledges for the first few days, then slow down or even flat-line for a woefully long period of time. If your campaign gets stalled for days, or if you didn't get off to a strong start in the first place, there are some things you can do.

SUPERCHARGE YOUR SOCIALS

Spread the word. Spread it like your favorite jam slathered on toast. Post regularly on your social media accounts, and don't forget to include the link to your campaign. I often see authors forget this essential part.

Make a fun video highlighting something about your campaign, and post it everywhere. Along with the link, of course.

What to post about?

Every goal you reach. Something cool about your book. Any unique selling points that would appeal to your readers. Your inspiration. The extra bonuses backers can get by supporting the project on Kickstarter.

Post regularly, but change things around. Show off pretty graphics one day. Talk about stretch rewards the next. Post a silly meme that's on point and stick your campaign link in the first comment. Keep being creative and upbeat.

Remind your newsletter

Unless you have built your newsletter specifically using Kickstarter campaigns, I don't recommend blasting out every other day to your newsletter. Weekly seems to be a good balance for most authors. Make sure you entice your readers and tell them why their support right now matters.

Update your web presences

Put your campaign information and graphics front and center on your website. Don't forget a big, obvious button that takes people to your project on Kickstarter.

Use your campaign banner as your Facebook banner. Don't forget to add your link in the first comment.

Update your bio buttons on all the platforms to link to your campaign.

Wherever you are on the web, make your project visible, along with a link for interested people to click through and check it out. Spreading awareness isn't the same thing as a hard sell. Invariably, when your campaign ends, you will have people tell you they had no idea you were running a Kickstarter.

TWEAK YOUR CAMPAIGN

Try some new things to get your project moving again. Maybe a different banner would help, or changing the order of your campaign story. If you're working toward a stretch goal, put that up top to entice new backers to jump in. Here's a list of things to consider:

- Refresh your banner.
- Take a hard look at your title and subtitle. Are they doing their job?
- Put your next, enticing Stretch Reward at the top of your campaign.
- Reorder your campaign. What if you led with the unlocked stretch rewards for a day, or the special edition features? Maybe a new image up top?
- Add a new reward tier, then post about it on your socials.
- Add a new add-on, then post about that, too.
- Add a video to your project if you didn't originally create one.

The beauty of Kickstarter is that we can keep tweaking and refining our campaigns. If something isn't working, try another thing. Just make sure to give your new changes a day or two to settle before you decide whether or not they're working.

TRY A FLASH REWARD

One way to get a stalled campaign moving again is with a flash reward. Pick something simple and inexpensive, or move one of your stretch rewards up. Rather than a funding goal, however, I recommend you set your flash reward goal to a backer count number. Give yourself a few days to reach the flash, and try to make it as attainable as possible.

I have used flash rewards twice to help jump-start a flatlined campaign. The first was a new character card that I'd been secretly holding in reserve for a stretch reward, and the second was a short story from my backlist.

All backers should receive the flash reward, not just new pledgers. Always treat your backers, especially your early ones, like the VIPs they are.

USE THE KICKSTARTER PLATFORM

In addition to changing things around in your campaign, there are some things you can do on Kickstarter that might help give you a visibility boost.

Back other campaigns in your genre, especially if you've only backed a small number. This has worked for a number of authors when their projects were stalled out. Something about backing other projects tickled the algorithms and got the platform to start showing their campaigns a little more widely.

Change your category on Kickstarter, if your campaign is a good fit for something more than the Fiction category.

Send an update to former backers, if you've run campaigns in the past, reminding them your most recent project is live.

CROSS-PROMOTE WITH OTHER CREATORS

One of the most powerful ways to boost your campaign is by trading mentions with other creators when you send a backer update. This is a time-honored strategy used by creators across the platform, and it makes sense. You're directly reaching people who are active on Kickstarter and have backed campaigns like yours.

Commonly referred to as backer swaps, creators agree to highlight one another's campaigns when they send out a backer update. Kickstarter adds other projects at the end of every update email. Why not give the book ecosystem a boost by highlighting other authors?

Unlike other platforms with more rigid ecosystems, backers on Kickstarter are allowed to have eclectic tastes. You don't have to share only campaigns that are in your precise genre. Backers are wonderfully omnivorous.

Recommendations also don't have to be on live-for-live campaigns. You will be staying in touch with backers for every campaign you run, and continuing to update them. Use your updates on ended campaigns to help spread the word for other authors, too. We tend to think of Kickstarter as only existing during our campaigns, but it's an active place where the people who backed our campaigns are still around, backing other projects. As authors, we can continue to create a robust ecosystem for book lovers on Kickstarter by spotlighting book projects in our post-campaign updates.

It's a best practice to generously swap campaign mentions with other Kickstarter creators. Ideally, every update you send would include three to four other campaigns. You can reach out directly to other creators asking to cross promote. Even better, join the (Experienced) Kickstarter for Authors Cross-promotion group on Facebook, which is specifically set up to facilitate this kind of cross-promotion.

CANCELLED PLEDGES

One of the things that can make your campaign feel stuck is when backers cancel their pledges. It can be frustrating to feel like you're going one step forward and one back and getting nowhere.

Backers can and do cancel their pledges. It's just part of how Kickstarter works. A pledge is not a purchase, and it's important for authors to get out of the mindset that it is.

Don't take it personally when a backer cancels their pledge. Life happens. As creators, we can't know what a backer's personal situation might be. They might have run into an unexpected financial situation. They might have just changed their mind.

Plan on having some cancelled pledges. It's okay. In the end, you will likely regain that ground. Plus, you'll know that every backer you have at the end of the campaign is there to support you and is excited about what you have to offer.

MAINTAIN YOUR SANITY

Running a campaign can be emotionally taxing. Pace yourself. Maybe you only have so much bandwidth. Maybe your skillset isn't coming up with hooky social media messages or thinking up a bunch of extra rewards for your campaign.

If you have already hit your funding goal, maybe you don't need to worry if your campaign slows to a trickle. If that feels right to you, plan a few more social media posts, update your backers as needed, and give yourself permission to coast into the end of your successful campaign.

I'm a "do all the things" person, and my advice here reflects that. But there's no one true way. We are on the hamster wheel so much in indie publishing. Kickstarter doesn't need to be that. There's enough stress in running a campaign that you don't have to pile on more. Find what works for you.

WHEN TO CONSIDER CANCELLING YOUR CAMPAIGN

For the most part, I recommend that creators with struggling campaigns stay the course. In some cases, though, you might realize early on that your campaign isn't going to work. Maybe your funding reach far exceeded your grasp. Maybe a family emergency has come up. Maybe it's halfway through the campaign and you only have four backers.

If you feel you need to cancel, communicate clearly with your backers about why. If you plan to restart the campaign right away, perhaps with a more realistic funding goal or timeline, let them know.

Alternatively, there's no shame in letting your campaign end unsuccessfully. Plenty of creators don't succeed the first time out.

Balance the pros and cons of your own sanity and energy. Whether you end up cancelling your Kickstarter campaign or just letting it roll out to the end, try not to take an unsuccessfully funded project as a personal failure. Learning the ins and outs of this platform is hard. If your project ends without reaching your funding goal, I encourage you to take a breath and try again.

CHAPTER 17
CROSSING THE FINISH LINE

- Last Promo Pushes
- Strategize Final Stretches
- Show Off Your Stuff
- Consider "Ending Soon" on Your Banner
- Final Follower Reminders from Kickstarter
- Grab Your Advanced Analytics
- Note Your Add-ons
- Tidy Up Your Campaign
- Confetti Time!
- What if the Distance Is Too Far?

The last three to four days of your campaign can be a busy time. You're entering the final phase of your Kickstarter, and it's important to take stock of how things are going. Do you need to make a big final push to reach your funding goal or last stretch reward? What can you do to bring your project home as successfully as possible?

Plan to lean on your promo. Be strategic about your last bonuses and stretch rewards/goals. Take advantage of the fact that Kickstarter will email everyone who is following but has not yet backed your campaign. And get ready for a final countdown with confetti!

LAST PROMO PUSHES

Now's the time to go hard on your social media and newsletter. Let people know they are about to miss out on your awesome book project. Lean on the time-limited nature of Kickstarter. Highlight the extra goodies and bonus rewards that are exclusive to your project. Activate people's FOMO and get them on board with your campaign!

STRATEGIZE FINAL STRETCHES

If you have a final reward or goal you'd like to reach before the end of the campaign, figure out a way to make it attainable. Change the target dollar amount to a backer number. If you've already unlocked all your campaign goodies, consider adding in a final bonus to entice fence-sitters to pledge. Go out strong!

SHOW OFF YOUR STUFF

Before the forty-eight-hour mark, I like to move all my unlocked stretches and bonus rewards to the top of my campaign page. Make a nice graphic showing the unlocked rewards. Seeing all the extra goodies that are now in the campaign can motivate followers to stop looking and start pledging. In particular, emphasize which rewards are exclusive to backers and will not be available once the campaign ends.

CONSIDER "ENDING SOON" ON YOUR BANNER

While Kickstarter doesn't encourage creators to add extra text or badges to their banners, it can be helpful to add a final countdown or "ending soon" message to your banner for the last few days of your campaign. I have done this on three of my campaigns. While I don't have specific evidence that it worked, I don't have evidence that it didn't, either.

FOLLOWER REMINDER EMAILS FROM KICKSTARTER

Forty-eight hours before your campaign ends, Kickstarter sends out an email to followers who are watching your campaign but have not yet backed. I spotlight my unlocked rewards and bonuses at the top of my campaign before that crucial moment. I want followers who come back to look at the project page to see all the extras they'll get if they support, and what they'll miss out on forever if they don't.

Kickstarter sends another email to followers at the eight-hour mark before your campaign ends.

Ideally, you'll see some "end spike" pledges as a result of these emails and the tweaking you've done to entice those followers to become backers. Be aware that a low rate of conversion from followers to backers is normal on Kickstarter. Ten to 30% isn't unusual. Campaigns with over 50% of followers converting to backers is excellent and fairly unusual. It's more common with smaller or niche campaigns. Be prepared for the reality, so it doesn't come as a surprise or disappointment if you're expecting higher conversion numbers.

GRAB YOUR ADVANCED ANALYTICS

Once your campaign ends, you will no longer see the link to your Advanced Analytics from your project page dashboard. Download those metrics if you'd like to have them handy.

There's currently a workaround to the disappearing analytics. Before your campaign ends, go to your Advanced Analytics page and copy the URL. Stash that web address someplace safe. With it you can access your analytics even after the campaign has ended. At least until Kickstarter closes this loophole.

NOTE YOUR ADD-ONS

Oddly, once your campaign ends, you have no way to see the add-ons section of your project. You'll be able to see which add-ons backers added to their pledge, and the add-ons will appear in the fulfillment section. If you titled an add-on something like "Super Special Swag Pack," you'll need to copy down everything that you included in that add-on. Otherwise, on the backer report, you'll see that someone pledged for "Super Special Swag Pack" but there's no break-down of the specific items included. You'll see all your items listed out in your fulfillment section, but those aren't broken down by backer. Save yourself a headache and make sure you know exactly what items are included as part of each add-on.

TIDY UP YOUR CAMPAIGN

Once your campaign ends, you can no longer edit any part of the story. Take the last half-hour of your campaign to make any final tweaks or changes to how the project will appear in perpetuity.

If you put "ending soon" information on your banner, it will stay that way unless you replace it before your campaign ends. Same with the stretch rewards up top or any other changes you made to try to encourage those final-days backers.

Many creators like to tidy up and put their campaigns back to their original state before the clock runs out.

CONFETTI TIME!

Make sure you watch the final few minutes of your campaign on your Kickstarter project page itself, not on your dashboard. There's an adrenaline-spiking countdown in the final seconds. And once you end, there's confetti!

Congratulations. You ran a successful campaign. I hope you have a celebration planned.

WHAT IF THE DISTANCE IS TOO FAR?

If you are almost at the end of your campaign and have funded less than 50% of your goal, success might be out of reach this time around. However, I have seen a very few campaigns in this range make a Herculean push and reach their funding goal. It took the help of a lot of community support and relentlessly spreading the word. If you're not up for that level of effort, that's fine. Remember, 60% of Kickstarter campaigns do not fund.

Resist the urge to cancel your campaign at this late date. Kickstarter backers understand that not every project succeeds. Let your project run its course, then try again, using what you've learned.

CHAPTER 18
POST-CAMPAIGN

- Errored Pledges
- Button Redirect
- Victory Update
- Reward Surveys
- Receiving Your Funds

Your campaign's over, but there's still plenty of work ahead. Before you start worrying about reward fulfillment, there are a few things you need to take care of. Check for errored pledges. Send a celebratory backer update. Let your backers know what's next. Gear up for fulfillment by prepping your backer surveys. And, most importantly, receive your funds from Kickstarter!

ERRORED PLEDGES

Sometimes a credit card doesn't go through when Kickstarter charges the backer at the end of your campaign. Their card might have expired, or if they're a first-time backer, their credit card company might have flagged the charge from Kickstarter. As soon as your campaign ends, you'll want to check your backer report for errored pledges. Those show as a red exclamation mark by the backer's name. You can also find errored pledges by sorting your backers. Click the "all backers" dropdown menu on your backer report. "Errored backers" will be shown high up on the list. If you don't see either red exclamation marks or dropped backers, then you have no errored pledges. Yay!

It's not uncommon to have errored pledges, especially with a bigger campaign. Kickstarter will reach out every forty-eight hours to remind backers to fix their pledge details. Most of the errored pledges will resolve in the first few days.

However, it's important to know that **if a backer does not fix their credit card details within seven days after the end of your project, Kickstarter will permanently drop them from your campaign**.

On about day four, I start reaching out directly to backers who still have unresolved pledges. Not only do I message them via Kickstarter, I email them directly. Sometimes backers are unaware that there's an issue. Make sure to tell them that Kickstarter will drop them from your campaign if they can't fix their pledge. Give them the specific date they will be removed, and tell them you'd hate for them to miss out on the rewards they pledged for. I offer backers the opportunity to pay me off-platform if they can't get their credit card details resolved in time. A PayPal invoice usually works well for this.

The day before the backer is about to be dropped, I email them directly one last time. I've been able to recover the majority of my errored pledges this way, but sometimes you never hear back and that pledge is lost forever. Again, it's just one of the things that happens. Out of my eight campaigns, seven of them lost some backers due to errored pledges.

BUTTON REDIRECT AND PAGE CUSTOMIZATION

As soon as your campaign ends, you have the option to make a few changes to how your project page appears on Kickstarter.

The most important thing is that Kickstarter allows you to turn the Pledge button into a linked button that redirects elsewhere. Use this to send people to where they can get your book, either in preorder or via a "late pledge." Creators often link to the book's preorder page or their direct store, or take late pledges via a Google sheet order form or a third-party pledge manager.

In addition to redirecting the button, you can also customize the background color and text on your campaign page, add a new banner image, and edit your title and subtitle. However, the Story itself can't be changed.

VICTORY UPDATE

Keep that final celebration momentum going by sending out a big "hooray, we did it!" update thanking all your backers. Include a rough timeline of what happens next. Remind backers when to expect their rewards, and let them know when you plan to send out the reward surveys. (I usually wait at least a week before sending backer surveys to give errored pledges a chance to resolve.)

If you are in need of time-sensitive information, like backers' names to go into a book's thank-you section, make sure people are aware of the deadline. Creators often include a link to a Google sheet where backers can add the name they'd like to have appear in the acknowledgements. It's not always their Kickstarter handle.

If you have several errored pledges, mention something along these lines in your update: "X number of backers have errored pledges, which means there's an issue with the payment details on Kickstarter. Please double-check your credit card details. I'd hate for you to miss out on the rewards you pledged for!"

If you have an order sheet or store where backers can pick up extras or add-ons, make sure to put the link in your update.

REWARD SURVEYS

The next step in prepping for fulfillment is sending out reward surveys to your backers. You do this in the Pledge Management section of your project page dashboard. Click on "reward surveys." An interface will open showing you each tier with the number of backers. You will need to create a new survey for each reward tier. (Copy/paste can be your friend here.) When creating the survey, you have the ability to add a number of question fields to make sure you have all the information you need from your backer.

Be aware that you can only send a survey **once** to a tier. Create a rough draft and let it sit for a day or two, to make sure you haven't left anything out before hitting the send button.

When to send out your surveys

As mentioned above, I generally wait at least a week before sending surveys. However, if you have no errored pledges and you're eager to get started, by all means send out your surveys.

There are times when you might want to delay sending out a survey. If you have a longer delivery time (several months or more after the close of the campaign) people's addresses may change and they might forget to update their Kickstarter information. Some game campaigns I've backed haven't sent the surveys out until right before they ship the rewards (which could be over a year) to make sure they have the most up-to-date shipping address.

You don't need to send all surveys to all tiers at the same time. If your digital rewards are ready to go, get those reward surveys out to backers right away.

What to include in your backer survey

Open with a thank you! Your project wouldn't exist without the support of your backers. After that, add a brief overview of your rewards fulfillment timeline for that specific tier. You might want to add a sentence or two giving a certain number of months for backers to fill out the survey and claim their rewards before they're donated elsewhere. Sometimes backers don't return their surveys (or respond to repeated email requests) for months, or even years, after the campaign closes. You can't be expected to hold their rewards indefinitely, or until they finally get back to you. State your policy and be clear there's a finite response-time window.

If the survey is going out to a tier that included physical items, Kickstarter automatically adds required address fields. You can give backers the option to edit their address, which I generally do.

You have the option to add multiple-choice or text questions, and to make these optional or required. I usually add the following, depending on what I've offered in the campaign:

- Best email address to deliver digital rewards. (required)
- What name they'd like their books signed to, if that was included in the campaign. (required, with an instruction to write n/a if they only want the book autographed but not personalized)
- How they'd like their name to appear in the thank-you section of the book. (required, again with an n/a instruction if they don't want their name to appear)
- A multiple-choice question asking if they'd like to join my mailing list (yes, no, already on it). (optional)
- A text question asking if there are any questions or comments. (optional)

In addition, use your survey to clarify which options the backer wants, if the tier offered some choices. This is particularly important in the case of things like T-shirts, alternate cover versions, a choice of books, etc.

Update your backers

As soon as your reward surveys are sent out, make an update letting people know. Remind backers that you'll need their information in order to start delivering rewards. You might also want to add the same bit about lack of response after X number of months means the rewards will be donated.

Don't forget to cross-promote other authors' Kickstarter campaigns at the end of every update.

A surge, then a trickle

Most backers will return their surveys to you right away. Some will trickle in a week or two down the line. In some cases, you'll need to message and direct email a backer to get their shipping information so you can deliver their rewards. Some backers you will never hear back from.

RECEIVING YOUR FUNDS

You should receive your campaign funds from Kickstarter, via electronic funds transfer into your bank account, roughly two weeks after your campaign ends. If you ended on a weekend or evening, some banks might take a few extra days to make the transfer. Bank holidays slow things down, too. If it has been three weeks and you don't yet have your funds, reach out to Kickstarter support. They will help sort out any problems you might have with your bank or payment details.

CHAPTER 19
FULFILLMENT

- Fulfillment Section
- Rely on Your Backer Report
- Delivering Rewards
- Unreturned Surveys
- Reward Status
- Transparency
- Final Update
- Download Your Report
- What's Next?

Once your campaign money is in your account and you're getting surveys returned from backers, you can start fulfilling your rewards! Provided they're ready, of course. You can begin fulfilling your campaign earlier, but most creators prefer to wait until they have payment in hand, especially when it comes to shipping out physical rewards.

Kickstarter provides some tools to help with fulfillment tracking. In general, the downloadable reports are either too basic or too unwieldy to be highly useful without a lot of tweaking by the user. Many creators find them quite frustrating. There's a reason for the flourishing third-party pledge manager ecosystem.

That said, I've found the Kickstarter interface usable enough so far. I encourage you to give it a try for at least one campaign and see how it works for you. And it's free!

FULFILLMENT SECTION

At the bottom of your Pledge Management section on your project page dashboard is a "Fulfillment" link. Clicking that will open up a fairly simple page with some graphs showing what percentage of backers have returned their surveys and how much of your campaign is fulfilled to date. (Skip over the Easyship section up top. Although they have a partnership with Kickstarter to help with shipping, it's not yet ready for prime time, according to the authors who have used it.)

The most useful information on this page is at the bottom, under "Reward items." Kickstarter has tallied up the numbers of each individual reward item across your pledges and add-ons. The dashboard here will show you exactly how many copies of your books, and in which formats, you will need to fulfill all your pledges.

WARNING: This number does not take into account any dropped pledges. If you had someone pledge for all your hardcovers but then they are dropped from your campaign, those hardcover orders will still appear here in your fulfillment dashboard. Make sure to cross-check the item numbers and adjust for any pledges that are no longer a part of your campaign.

Always order extra copies of your physical books, however. There's nothing more frustrating than ordering the exact number you need only to have two of them misprinted and one with shipping damage. Give yourself some wiggle room so you won't have to keep backers hanging while you reorder their books.

RELY ON YOUR BACKER REPORT

Once your reward surveys start coming in, those backers' records in the backer report table will update with the answers to your survey questions. Even more importantly, the record displays exactly what tier and add-ons each backer pledged for. In fact, the only place you can easily see this information is by clicking a backer's name in the backer report. There is no single, super-clear spreadsheet that displays this information (not without a lot of sorting and deleting unnecessary columns), and no "packing list"-type report available for you to print out.

I work directly off the backer report when fulfilling rewards. Not only can I see at a glance what each backer's reward items are, I can leave myself a note on their record and update their status to "in progress" or "shipped" as appropriate. Once most of the surveys are in, I sort by tiers and work through them methodically. You can message all backers of any given tier. So, once a tier's rewards are fulfilled, I send a message to let all the backers know. (I also send out an update around the same time, to make sure backers know where I am in the fulfillment process, in case they didn't see the tier message.)

It might seem tedious, as opposed to being able to hit a button and load all that information into a nice template, but that's the current limitation of the Kickstarter system. It's workable. But if the thought of working directly from the backer report online gives you hives, you can look into a third-party pledge management company.

DELIVERING REWARDS

As an author, you'll be fulfilling two types of book rewards: digital and physical.

Digital Rewards

For eBooks, the current gold standard for delivery is Book-Funnel. You will need to make a paid account. This will allow you to send your backers their eBooks any number of ways. Many authors create a landing page and send backers the link to go get their rewards. Bulk delivery into a backer's digital library is becoming an increasingly popular option. And finally, you can email the download link directly to the backer. There are pros and cons to each delivery method, and no one way to do it. Reach out to other authors who have done this before, and figure out what feels best to you.

In addition to eBooks, BookFunnel can also host audiobooks and smaller-sized PDFs. I've used BookFunnel for both character art and coloring page delivery, as well as eBooks.

If you don't want to use BookFunnel, you might host digital files on your website or deliver them to backers via Dropbox.

Physical Rewards

While researching your campaign, you should have figured out your various shipping options.

Give yourself enough time to package and ship your rewards, if you have them on hand, or to get them printed and shipped if you're drop-shipping. Refer to the sections on shipping in Chapter Four for more tips. In particular, watch out for end-of-the-year holiday delays in both printing and shipping.

UNRETURNED SURVEYS

Some backers will never return their surveys. If a digital-only backer doesn't respond by fulfillment time, I use their Kickstarter email to deliver their rewards and then mark them as complete. But without a mailing address, it's impossible to mail out physical rewards.

If you've made every effort to contact a backer, both via message and direct email, and are unable to deliver their rewards, you will not be in trouble. Kickstarter understands that this happens.

REWARD STATUS

On your backer report you have the ability to mark the status of a backer's pledge. Your options are: not started, in progress, shipped, and delayed. These can be marked individually in the backer's record. Alternatively, you can select a number of backers on the main backer report page and have the option to change all the selected statuses at once.

As soon as you begin fulfillment, mark the appropriate backers and tiers as "in progress." Once the rewards have been delivered, make sure to change that status to "shipped."

Kickstarter uses this to track the percentage of your rewards that have been fulfilled. They generally will not approve a new campaign from you until most of your previous campaign rewards have been fulfilled.

It's important to keep the reward status up to date so that backers can see where you are in regards to delivering their rewards. If they are marked as "shipped" but haven't received anything, ideally they will reach out to you to see what happened with their rewards.

TRANSPARENCY

If any delays or issues arise, make sure to let your backers know right away. Use the campaign's updates ability to do this. If a backer reaches out to Kickstarter, they will be able to see that you've publicly addressed the issue. (Something that Kickstarter is big on.)

Even if you don't have much to report, send a backer update every month, give or take. Reassure your supporters you're working on their rewards. Show off some in-progress pictures of your book or new artwork. Make sure backers know you haven't forgotten about them or their promised rewards.

FINAL UPDATE

Once you've sent out the very last rewards, it's essential you make a final, public-facing update on your campaign. This is the cherry on top. Thank your backers once again. Let them know that ALL rewards are out and they should contact you if they didn't get their goodies.

Kickstarter is looking for that transparent, public-facing closure and proof that their system is working as intended. About 9% of Kickstarter creators never deliver their rewards. Kickstarter wants to know—and wants anyone reading your campaign updates to know—that you have fulfilled your rewards and are a trustworthy creator. The more obvious it is on the platform that the vast majority of projects deliver as promised, the better it is for the entire ecosystem. Plus, the more obvious it is that you are delivering on your promises, the better it is for you.

Finally, don't forget to double-check that you've marked all delivered rewards as "Shipped."

DOWNLOAD YOUR BACKER REPORT

The backer information expires a year after you originally indicated in your campaign that all rewards would be delivered. If you still need any of that information, download a copy of the backer report.

WHAT'S NEXT?

Ideally, another Kickstarter project!

You can be working on a new campaign at any point in time. Maybe you started drafting a new one right after you launched your current project, or maybe you've been working behind the scenes on several at once.

Once you've fulfilled your rewards, you can put your next project in for approval. Most of the time, Kickstarter will approve it for prelaunch. If they do not, make sure you've marked your items as "Shipped" in the backer status, and double-check that you made that final, public-facing update that all rewards are out to backers.

Kickstarter will not approve a project while you have one currently live, or if you haven't done any reward fulfillment on your last campaign.

Once you've successfully run and fulfilled four campaigns in the Publishing category, you are considered a "creator in good standing." At that point, you're allowed to have a few campaigns in various stages. Currently, I have one in prelaunch and two that are in fulfillment. However, you are never allowed to have two projects live at the same time.

If you loved running your campaign, I hope you keep using the platform regularly!

Or not...

After the dust has settled and you've had a chance to evaluate the entire process, maybe you'll end up feeling that Kickstarter isn't for you. That's perfectly fine. Some creators find the platform really doesn't work for them, for a variety of reasons. Maybe your time is better spent writing the next book. Maybe the stress was too over the top. Maybe crowdfunding just isn't your jam.

Still, I hope that using Kickstarter for your book project brought you some tangible and intangible rewards. You've made some new fans. Created beautiful books. Launched your book with profit, or at least defrayed expenses.

My wish for every author reading this book is that, by running a Kickstarter campaign, you've gained a new level in your career. Whatever your path going forward, congratulate yourself on all you've learned. You're an indie author, and that means control over your career is *yours*.

Onward and upward!

CHAPTER 20
KICKSTARTER AND YOUR CAREER

- How Many Campaigns a Year?
- Keeping Your Backers on Board
- Building Your Success

If you've embraced using Kickstarter as part of your long-term career strategy, it's good to be, well, strategic about it.

This means pacing yourself, being smart about what you're offering, not oversaturating your backers, and being ready for some inevitable ups and downs.

HOW MANY CAMPAIGNS A YEAR?

Some creators run multiple campaigns a year. Some plan a big yearly project. Others might use Kickstarter less regularly, depending on what else is going on in their lives.

If you're ready to do three or more campaigns a year, make sure you familiarize yourself with the best months to run a project on Kickstarter. This info is in Oriana Leckert's interview, included in this book, and elsewhere. This will change as the book ecosystem matures, so use what you learn as a guideline. There are always exceptions to the rule. And again, the platform is your best teacher. Notice how book campaigns are performing throughout the year, and make your choices based on that data.

Give yourself enough time between planned campaigns to get your rewards out. I've been stretched trying to fulfill two campaigns at once, and I don't recommend it.

I run about four campaigns a year. Two of them are "bigger" in terms of being more special hardcover editions. I'll space those out about six months apart, one in the spring and one in the fall. I will keep making less ambitious campaigns, too, to fill in between those big ones. A paperback short story collection is a nice refresher, for both me and my backers. A "different" project can be a fun way to switch things up, too. So far I've explored the world of art books and nonfiction. Poetry is probably next (my first love, actually).

Take stock of your planned book releases and how you'd like to use Kickstarter. If you plan to launch every new release first on the platform, then that will dictate your timing. If you have a big anniversary coming up, that will give you something to plan for.

Whatever you do, pace yourself. Some people are energized by using Kickstarter, and running four campaigns a year is just fun. Others need to dial it back a bit. There's no one right way.

KEEPING YOUR BACKERS

I think it's important not to oversaturate your backers. You don't necessarily want to hit them up for a high-end hardcover every couple months, for example. Switching between series and genres can help keep your catalog fresh and interesting. Strike a balance between frontlist and backlist, and between big projects and smaller ones.

As you use Kickstarter and run more campaigns, you'll get a feel for who your core supporters are. You'll get to know what kinds of extra things they like, and you will be able to give them even more of that in successive campaigns. Heck, go ahead and send a Google survey, polling your backers about what they'd like to see for your next campaign! This is a collaborative space, after all.

There's a tricky balance to building a campaign that will have something for all your supporters. Physical and digital. New fans and longtime supporters. People with small budgets and those who love to spend big money on books. Consider all your stakeholders any time you're putting together a new campaign, and do your best to include a tier that will delight them.

BUILDING YOUR SUCCESS

There's a build on Kickstarter, although it might not always feel linear. Even if it's not a financial build, you will continue to grow your supporters and your campaign skills. You may, like several creators I've known, start with a decently successful project, then have a lackluster second campaign, then come roaring back and knock it out of the park on your third or fourth project.

But don't force yourself to keep doing campaigns if you hate every minute and your experience is full of stress and exhaustion. Be good to yourself.

What if you're not seeing a build on Kickstarter?

It's possible that you've done a few campaigns and aren't actually seeing upward momentum in terms of funding higher or getting more backers.

While it can be common to have a second campaign falter, or a third, if you're seeing a flatline or a downward trend, you might need to ask yourself a few questions.

Are you doing campaigns for similar books in close succession?

Maybe you're tapping your audience too frequently. Try switching things up. Put out a title in a different series or genre, do a backlist omnibus or collection, or switch to a frontlist release.

Are you delivering to expectations, and above?

Make sure that you're providing great value to your backers. This doesn't mean you have to include blingy swag (although that can be fun for some creators). Are your prices in line with the current norm on Kickstarter? If higher, what extras are you delivering to your backers to make them feel delighted that they supported you?

Did you exhaust your backlist?

For authors with big backlists, there can be diminishing returns if you're offering your entire backlist with every campaign. A lot of happy book backers will scoop those up on campaign one, giving you a nice, high-flying fund. But in subsequent campaigns, your core supporters won't be grabbing those big book bundles in high-dollar tiers. They already have everything.

At that point, your job is to make your new campaigns as enticing as possible. Especially if you're creating hardcovers, make sure you're adding all those extra touches. Custom chapter headers. Under-jacket case design that's different from the front cover. Maybe illustrations, two-page art spreads, etc. There's a lot you can do even with POD to make your books extra-appealing to your supporters.

Save something for later.

Be strategic about your long-term plans for using Kickstarter. You want to have some nice, high-level tiers in each campaign, and backlist is great for that, but maybe don't offer everything in every campaign. Think about what you can keep in reserve to give oomph to another project down the line.

PART FOUR
RESOURCES AND NITTY-GRITTY

SHIPPING (AGAIN)

- What You Will Need to Calculate Shipping
- Mailing Books Yourself vs. Drop-Shipping
- Shipping Internationally

Even though we covered shipping in Chapter Four, it's something that worries a lot of authors. Therefore, here's that information again.

International creators, I have some different advice for you in the section for non-US creators, although if you're using a third-party distributor in the U.S. this section is worth a read.

WHAT YOU WILL NEED TO CALCULATE SHIPPING

A good digital scale. I actually have two: a kitchen scale that's accurate to about five pounds, and a regular scale that's good for heavier items.

Your shipping materials. You'll need samples of what you're going to be shipping your books in. Boxes, padded envelopes, bubble wrap, crinkle paper, etc.

Books. If you don't have copies of your books, then use some that are the same dimensions/weights as the books you're planning on shipping.

An account with one of the shipping consolidators. Pirate Ship is highly recommended, as they offer an excellent Simple Export Rate for international packages under four pounds. Ship Station and Easyship are also solid choices.

Sample addresses. Use your personal address book, or look up corporate or "dummy" addresses online for a variety of shipping destinations.

An understanding of Media Mail. Books can be sent via USPS Media Mail, which is the cheapest option around. Per the U.S. Postal Service rules, "Incidental First-Class Mail matter may be enclosed in or attached to any Media Mail piece without payment of First-Class Mail postage. An incidental First-Class Mail attachment or enclosure must be matter that, if mailed separately, would require First-Class Mail postage, is closely associated with but secondary to the host piece, and is prepared so as not to interfere with postal processing."

Many authors feel comfortable sending bookmarks and other book-related paper swag as "incidental matter." When in doubt, take your materials down to your local post office and ask them what they think. Anything you enclose needs to be related enough to the book to not cause issue. I'm guessing that non-paper swag would likely not meet the "closely associated with but secondary to the host piece" part of the rules.

A mug or keychain, for example, likely wouldn't count. Again, I am not an expert on USPS rules. Ask your local postmaster for guidance.

The postal service sometimes checks packages sent via Media Mail to make sure they are compliant with the rules. While you could be charged with mail fraud, the most common consequence of incorrectly using Media Mail is that your package is delivered with postage due to the recipient, charged at expensive Priority Mail rates.

MAILING BOOKS OUT YOURSELF VERSUS DROP-SHIPPING

To begin, you must decide whether you'll be handling your books yourself or having a POD printer do it for you via drop-shipping. There is a third option, which is to hire a third-party fulfillment company. This is something to consider if you know you'll be fulfilling orders for hundreds of books. It's generally not necessary for most authors, especially with a first-time campaign.

Handling your books yourself.

If you are planning to autograph your books, include swag, or create fancy book boxes, you will need to have your books sent to you from the printer. This is true whether your books are offset printed or POD.

Once you receive your books, you'll need to process them, package them, and mail the rewards out to individual backers. Don't forget to include the costs of your shipping materials. Boxes, packing tape, envelopes, and bubble wrap aren't free.

Drop-shipping.

One of the advantages of POD projects is that you can have the printer—Ingram, Lulu, Bookvault, or KDP—print and mail the books directly to each individual backer. This can save you a lot of time and hassle, but you won't be able to autograph the books or add swag to the package. For the best of both worlds, some authors drop-ship books from the printer and then send signed bookplates and swag separately.

Most offset printers don't drop-ship. These printers need to ship the entire order to one address. If you don't want to personally handle packaging and shipping each book reward, you'll need to hire a third-party fulfillment company. They will receive your boxes of books, package them for each order, and mail them to your backers. These companies charge a fee per order on top of shipping. If your campaign is wildly successful and you're looking at sending out hundreds or thousands of books, a third-party fulfillment company can help preserve your sanity.

Note: Third-party pledge managers, like BackerKit and PledgeBox, do *not* assist with physical fulfillment. They will not package or mail your books for you. There are also no printers "integrated" with Kickstarter. You'll need to figure out how to get your rewards to your backers.

Calculating the postage.

To figure out the cost of mailing out your books yourself, you'll need to know the weight of your packages. A kitchen scale is an essential tool. Don't forget to include the weight of the packing materials and any extra swag you're sending. You also need to know the dimensions of your box. These are often printed on the bottom.

Once you know your weight and the dimensions of your package, calculate the shipping via a free shipping consolidator company. Many authors prefer Pirate Ship, although Easyship and Ship Station are also popular choices. These companies provide discounts on shipping from USPS, FedEx, and UPS. You can pay for and print labels at home, and sometimes even arrange for your boxes to be picked up. Even though these companies cannot further discount USPS Media Mail (the cheapest way of shipping books within the U.S.), you can still pay for and print the labels using these services. If you are only sending books (and possibly paper swag), consider using Media Mail.

When calculating U.S. shipping, choose a state that's far from your own to get an idea of what your highest shipping costs might be.

Finally, if you are figuring out costs for a campaign that might not ship for several months, be aware that postage costs could rise during the interim. Verify your shipping right before your campaign goes live. You might also want to add a cushion, or consider charging shipping after your campaign ends, via a pledge manager like PledgeBox or BackerKit.

If you are drop-shipping from a POD printer, use their online price calculators to arrive at your shipping costs. Make sure to double-check right before your campaign goes live to see whether prices have changed.

Include the cost of your shipping materials (boxes, mailers, bubble wrap, etc.) in your shipping cost estimates.

Finally, don't forget to add on that extra 10% for Kickstarter and credit card fees.

SHIPPING INTERNATIONALLY

You don't *have* to offer physical books to international back-ers. You could choose to leave the rewards shipping on Kick-starter set to U.S. only. Some authors put a note in their campaign asking international backers to send a message if they're interested in getting print books. If there's a supporter in another country who wants to pledge, you can figure out the shipping just to their country and add that into your tiers.

Just be aware you will be leaving money on the table if you don't open your physical rewards to international backers.

One of the things that stops U.S. creators from offering print books outside the U.S. is the cost of overseas shipping. It's much more expensive than we are used to. But international backers are used to paying high shipping costs. Ask any Australian about international shipping to their country—for anything, not just Kickstarter rewards—and you'll be amazed at how much they have to pay.

In addition to high shipping fees, there are often questions about VAT, customs, and overseas taxes. For the most part, these are not as fraught as you might think. Many creators add shipping disclaimers for international backers in their campaign. It's a good idea to make international backers aware they might have to pay additional fees to receive their rewards, and that those fees and taxes will be their respon-sibility.

The advantage of using a POD printer and drop-shipping your book directly to backers is that most POD companies have printing facilities overseas. Shipping directly from Ingram UK or Bookvault UK to an address in the U.K. can cost the same as, or even less than, sending a book in the U.S.

from a U.S. printer. The countries that generally have higher shipping costs are Australia and Canada, so make sure to keep an eye on anything you plan to ship to those destinations. However, if you are using Lulu to print your books, they have facilities worldwide. Although their cost to print is high, their international drop-shipping rates can be amazingly low.

If you are drop-shipping and then sending out paper swag or signed bookplates, don't forget to check the international postage rates. Letters under one ounce are currently $1.50 to send from the U.S. to over 180 countries worldwide. Watch the weight, too. Once your letter goes over one ounce, the postage increases.

If you are not drop-shipping, but are personally sending signed books and swag out to international backers, things get a bit more complicated. Currently the easiest solution is to sign up with Pirate Ship and ask them for the Simple Export Rate option. This is the most competitive rate for overseas shipping. It is only available for U.S. creators, and the package must weigh less than four pounds.

All of the shipping companies help you with customs information and any extra fees you might be responsible for (generally, there are none). They make the process easy.

For packages over four pounds, you'll need to know your box weight and dimensions, and then use one of the shipping consolidator's calculators to see what the costs will be for various destinations.

You can find dummy addresses for international locations online, or look up international headquarters of various companies to get cities and codes to base your pricing on.

Canadian creators shipping from Canada might want to look into companies like Stallion Express and Chit Chats. They provide shipping solutions to the U.S., often cheaper than Canada Post.

Again, don't forget to include the cost of your shipping materials (boxes, mailers, bubble wrap, etc.) in your shipping. Most importantly, remember to add on that extra 10% for Kickstarter and credit card fees.

TAKEAWAY

There are some great shipping partners out there to help you, and some smart workarounds, like drop-shipping POD books from a printing facility and then sending signed bookplates separately, or using a simple export rate for international packages. Although it seems daunting at first, you can figure it out. After all, you've written entire books!

Customs can be a can of worms, but it doesn't need to be complicated, if you know how to address it correctly in your campaign and if you use a shipping partner that incorporates customs information on their shipping labels (as they almost all do).

PRINTERS: PRINT ON DEMAND COMPANIES

- Ingram
- Bookvault
- Amazon KDP
- Lulu
- A Note on ISBNs

Print on demand is a great way to keep your costs in line, since you're only paying to print one book at a time. However, it has its drawbacks in terms of special print features. Here's what you *can* do (depending on printer):

- Interior color. (Ingram, Bookvault, Lulu, KDP)
- Regular dust jackets. (Ingram, Bookvault UK, Lulu)
- Under-jacket case printing. (Ingram, Bookvault)
- Duplex covers (paperback only). (Ingram, Bookvault)
- Additional custom page added in front—Ingram only. (Good for digital signatures/personalizing drop-shipped copies, provided they do it correctly.)

And here's what you cannot do with Print on Demand:

- Foiled/embossed covers—with the exception of Bookvault, who are just about to roll out silver and gold foiling options! Be aware that a "block foiled" option is just the title and author name (text only) block-printed on the hardcover case. It's not fancy or customizable.
- Sprayed or stenciled edges. Again, keep an eye on Bookvault in the future. Also, some authors DIY or hire out sprayed edges after their book is POD printed.
- Endpapers.
- Ribboned bookmarks. However, Bookvault is rolling this out, too!
- Faux leather.
- Hubbed spines/head and tail bands.
- Smyth-sewn binding.
- White printing on black paper.
- Any other super-fancy special edition features.

For most of the above, you will need to do an actual print run. Some printers will take a low minimum of as few as fifty copies, but the fewer you print, the more expensive they will be. You're more likely looking at one to three hundred copies minimum.

Print on Demand companies. Currently, these are Ingram/LSI, Bookvault, Amazon KDP, and Lulu.

INGRAM

Ingram/LSI has recently restructured their costs and rolled out a few new options (premium color, a few more trim sizes, different paper options).

Pros:

No more up-front title setup cost.

If you select retail distribution, your print book will be available to libraries and a huge network of stores and bookstores (including Amazon).

You can use their internal SKU (not an ISBN) to create non-retailer copies that only you can order.

You can set preorders for your print books that will show up on all retailers.

Jacketed hardcovers.

Duplex covers.

Drop-shipping isn't terribly expensive to U.S./U.K./EU/AU.

Cons:

Customer service is notoriously hard to reach.

Slow printing and shipping times.

Some services can be unreliable (the customization option, notably).

Slow/confusing interface.

(Note: *Never* use Ingram to distribute your eBooks to other platforms. You lose a ton of control and there are so many better options out there! Check Draft2Digital if you want to use a distributor.)

BOOKVAULT

Bookvault is U.K.-based, but has recently partnered with a U.S. printing facility. Depending on where you get your books printed, there are different options and, of course, shipping variables. They are also a nimbler company, well aware of the needs of indie authors. Currently, Bookvault UK is on the cusp of being able to provide extras like gold and silver jacket foiling and custom slipcases for boxed sets. They also are hoping to offer sprayed edges in the future.

Pros:

Better print pricing than Ingram, in general (for orders placed with the U.K. printing facility).

Much better pricing for color, as they only charge per page, rather than entire book.

Ability to get your print book into U.K. distribution.

Jacketed hardcovers (but U.K. only at this point).

Duplex covers.

Drop-shipping isn't terribly expensive to U.S./U.K./EU.

Good customer service.

Integrates with direct sales platforms like Shopify.

You can use their internal SKU (not an ISBN) to create non-retailer copies that only you can order.

Cons:

Slow printing and shipping times, especially if your books are coming from the U.K.

U.S. facility doesn't currently provide all the trim sizes, or dustjackets for hardcovers.

U.S. prices aren't quite as competitive.

U.S. printer has had some ongoing quality control issues.

There's a fee to upload titles.

Slightly confusing interface.

Inability to completely digitally proof titles, so plan to order a proof copy—which could take a while to arrive.

AMAZON KDP

Amazon is generally the most competitive on print pricing, and sometimes on cost to drop-ship. However, there are some odd places you can't send books, like Switzerland. Some authors have run into problems shipping their author copies internationally to places like the U.K., too.

Pros:

Best print pricing for black-and-white interior books.

Drop-shipping isn't terribly expensive *if* you don't run into issues.

Gets your print book on Amazon with the best profit margin.

No title setup fee.

Cons:

Not all trim sizes supported.

No dustjackets for hardcovers.

Quality control can be random.

Printing/shipping times can be completely variable. (In August they were warning that author copies wouldn't arrive until October.)

LULU

Lulu actually has the fastest and least expensive worldwide drop-shipping capabilities. If you anticipate a lot of non-U.S. backers, you might want to investigate using them. The per-book cost will be higher, but the shipping fees could be much, much lower.

Pros:

Excellent drop-ship capabilities.

Very high-quality printing, especially in premium color.

Lulu storefront for your book (if you don't have a direct store).

No title setup fee.

Relatively fast, compared to the other POD companies.

You can use their internal SKU (not an ISBN) to create non-retailer copies that only you can order.

Cons:

Book printing costs are high.

Not all trim sizes supported.

They have a "distribution" option that's ridiculously expensive.

Almost all these printers have a cost calculator you can use to see how much your book will cost to print and ship. Check their websites for more information.

ISBNS

Most POD companies allow you to print books using an internal SKU, as long as you don't want to put your title into retail distribution. This is a great option if you're doing a Kickstarter-exclusive edition, or a title that will never be for sale at retailers.

PRINTERS: OFFSET PRINTING COMPANIES

- US
- CA
- UK
- AU
- China

Need more bells and whistles? Check out this *incomplete* list of offset print companies. Remember, offset printing requires a minimum print run, ranging from 50 (48hr Books) to 300 (SeSe) books. The more you order, the cheaper your per-book cost will be.

You can do more with offset printing than you can with POD printing. Authors commonly move to a print run in order to upgrade their books with the following:

- Foiled/embossed covers
- Sprayed or stenciled edges

- Endpapers
- Ribboned bookmarks
- Faux leather
- Hubbed spines/head and tail bands
- Smyth-sewn binding
- White printing on black paper
- Any other super-fancy special edition features

US-BASED PRINTERS:

Mixam

48hr Books

Bookmobile

Indie Author Book Services

(https://indieauthorprintondemand.com/)

Print Ninja

CANADIAN PRINTERS:

Sure Print & Design

https://sureprintanddesign.ca/

Mixam also has a CA arm

UK-BASED:

CPI Print

https://www.cpi-print.co.uk/

Clays

https://www.clays.co.uk/indie-publishing

Mixam also has a UK arm

AUSTRALIAN PRINTERS:

Kalligraphic

Mixam has an AU arm

CHINA:

Sese printing (Alibaba),

Rich Color http://www.richcolorprinter.com

The overseas printers will need a longer lead time for shipping your pallets of books to you. Definitely take that into account when planning how long your fulfillment will take.

There are a lot of printer options out there. This is only a small sampling. Do your research to find the best fit for your project.

ISSUES FOR CREATORS OUTSIDE THE U.S.

- Shipping
- VAT and taxes
- Currency Display
- US Backer Expectations

Running a Kickstarter from a location outside the US can be a challenge. For almost all campaigns, the majority of your backers will be located in the United States. This makes shipping more difficult and raises a number of issues, although there are a few work arounds. As a non-US creator, you'll also run into the currency display issue (Kickstarter shows rewards in your currency, not USD).

There are partial solutions to all these issues. It's always a good idea to be very clear in your campaign what the challenges might be, so that backers are aware.

SHIPPING

US backers are not used to high shipping costs the way the rest of the world is. There are some small ways you can work around this.

- Drop ship your books from a US-based POD printer. Send signed bookplates, or digitally sign your books.
- Hire a third-party fulfillment company in the US to receive your books from the printer. They will then package and ship to individual backers.
- Look into business mail programs with your local post office. If you're in Canada, you have a few more solutions – read on!

Shipping from Canada

Canada Post has a program for small businesses with some discount on shipping.

If you're in a large city you might be able to find a USPS shipping partner that will allow you to use media mail from Canada. If not, they're all just as expensive as each other, so Canada Post tends to be easiest. You'll need to pack the items yourself. You can either do the customs form online in the app or do it at the post office. Make sure to get insurance for the full value for your own peace of mind. Canada Post has up to $100 included in the price and it's cheap to add extra.

Stallion Express is one of those shipping partners that can ship via USPS and has locations in ON, PQ, and BC. Ask them about Media Mail.

There's apparently a similar service called Chitchats. Netparcel also might be worth looking into.

In the UK, check into business shipping with the Royal Mail.

Receiving boxes of books

In some countries, Canada included, see if you can self-clear your boxes at customs (usually this only works if you live in a big city). If you are working with an international printer, ask for door-to-door delivery service.

VAT AND TAXES

If you are a creator in the EU, you might be required to submit VAT (Value Added Tax). Consult your local accountant regarding the fees and taxes you're liable for. Kickstarter does not collect or remit any taxes on a creator's behalf.

CURRENCY DISPLAY

One of the more frustrating things for non-US creators is that your campaign displays your local currency. This cannot be changed. However, when your project is live, backers will see their own currency displayed as a smaller set of numbers.

If you live in a country that uses the dollar sign, but your currency is weaker than the dollar (AU and NZ especially) it would be wise to add something down near the bottom of your campaign about the exchange rate discrepancy. Reassure backers that while the numbers will fluctuate slightly, their pledge in X AUD will come out to roughly Y in USD.

US BACKER EXPECTATIONS

People in the US are not used to high international shipping rates. It's best to be as clear as possible about the added costs if you are mailing rewards from overseas. As ever on Kickstarter, transparent communication is always the best choice.

RESOURCES ON KICKSTARTER

CREATOR RESOURCES

Kickstarter Creator Resources are many and thorough! Definitely check them out!

Start with <u>Creator questions – Kickstarter Support</u>

(help.kickstarter.com/hc/en-us/categories/115000492154-Creator-questions)

Also check out the blog specific to Publishing:

Kickstarter Creator Tips: Publishing, Comics, and Journalism — Kickstarter

(kickstarter.com/creators/publishing)

For **budgeting,** definitely read this article by Russell Nohelty:

How to Create an Expert Kickstarter Budget (updates.kickstarter.com/how-to-create-an-expert-kickstarter-budget/)

BRAND ASSETS

Kickstarter provides branded assets for you to use in your graphics, including some social media badges and logos. They recommend this for promotion you're doing off Kickstarter, in particular.

Find those here: Brand assets — Kickstarter

(kickstarter.com/help/brand_assets)

KICKSTARTER'S BUILT-IN PARTNERSHIPS

- PledgeManager
- Easyship

Kickstarter has teamed up with a few companies in an attempt to make things easier for creators. However, the general consensus from creators who have used these companies in conjunction with their campaigns is that they are not quite ready for prime time. Ideally, this will change and there might eventually be seamless pledge management and shipping solutions integrated with the Kickstarter platform. But they're not there yet.

PLEDGEMANAGER

PledgeManager has ongoing issues with migrating campaign rewards and add-ons to their site. There is reportedly a great deal of human error on their end. Creators who have worked with them report being frustrated in general with the interface.

EASYSHIP

While at first glance the Easyship partnership seems like a great idea, there are several issues with it. The biggest one is that it's only available for US shipping. Creators especially struggle with international shipping, and it's too bad there isn't an elegant solution here.

Authors who are used to shipping books out with Easyship outside of Kickstarter have reported that the Kickstarter-based version is more expensive and way more complicated to use. There seem to be a number of bugs still to be worked out with the Kickstarter/Easyship interface. At this time, the current recommendation is to avoid this partnership. Sign up with Easyship yourself. Or better yet, check out Pirate Ship and their Custom Export Rate for international shipping.

BONUS ADVICE FROM KICKSTARTER SUPPORT

I asked one of the top support people at Kickstarter if they had any advice they'd like to impart to creators. Check out these words of wisdom.

"For projects that are about to launch, a big area of focus should be setting up a well-structured list of rewards/add-ons that are both enticing for backers and realistic for the creator. Basically, don't set unrealistic expectations, whether it's the turnaround time, shipping costs, etc. It can be a bit daunting, but putting in the work to research shipping costs and fulfillment ahead of the launch should be top of mind when setting up rewards and will pay dividends down the road."

RESOURCES OFF KICKSTARTER

- Third-Party Pledge Managers
- Third-Party Fulfillment Companies

THIRD-PARTY PLEDGE MANAGERS

So, what are these pledge management companies, and what can they do for you?

Back in the day, Kickstarter's fulfillment tools fell a bit short of creators' needs. A number of companies sprang up to help fill the gap. These are called pledge managers, and they can help you do the following:

- More easily organize your backers' information into useful spreadsheets.
- Charge shipping later, after your campaign has ended.
- Help you continue to take pledges for your rewards after your Kickstarter ends.

- Assist in recovering errored pledges more aggressively than Kickstarter does.
- Help with robust backer surveys.
- Help deliver digital rewards.
- Help you maintain a mailing list of your backers.

They cannot help you fulfill physical rewards, other than giving you good spreadsheets and helping you with shipping quotes (provided they are integrated with shipping companies).

Third-party pledge managers can also be difficult and frustrating to get set up, especially if your campaign is a bit more complex. (BackerKit is notorious for this.)

None of this is free. Some pledge managers, like BackerKit, take a percentage of your total campaign raise. Some, like PledgeBox, only take a percentage of anything you sell post-campaign via their platform. All of them charge a percentage for credit card fees.

My advice is, if you're running a smaller campaign, try using the tools that Kickstarter gives you before worrying about using a pledge manager. Kickstarter has spreadsheets and tables (though they can be frustrating to use). Kickstarter does try to recover errored pledges. The Kickstarter reward survey you send to backers is very robust. You should be maintaining your own newsletter (invite your backers to join). In fact, there are ways to self-provide almost all the above at no extra cost. The only exception is charging shipping after your campaign has ended. However, sometimes backers are not fans of being charged after the fact, especially if that was not made clear in the campaign or if the shipping charges are high.

If you want to continue to take "orders" after your campaign ends, consider setting up a Google Form as an order form, with your rewards listed there. That plus a PayPal invoice can take you far.

More authors are moving to direct stores. If you have the ability to sell direct, continue to offer your rewards and add-ons on your webstore.

Digital rewards can be easily delivered via BookFunnel.

Creators who have been using Kickstarter for a long time have gotten used to using pledge managers. However, Kickstarter has been working hard to improve their fulfillment tools and pledge management systems over the past few years. In general, I find the Kickstarter tools (spreadsheets, tables, reward surveys, and updates) to be more than adequate to the task.

If you'd like to explore what a third-party pledge manager can do for you, I recommend you research PledgeBox and BackerKit.

If you have a Shopify store, look into the Crowd Control app. This was built specifically by a Kickstarter user to provide a pledge-management interface with his Shopify store.

THIRD-PARTY FULFILLMENT COMPANIES

If you are running a big campaign, consider hiring a third-party fulfillment company. These companies will take delivery of your boxes of printed books and repack them to send out to individual backers. For a fee, of course. This list is incomplete. Always get quotes and do your due diligence.

Merrick Books – highly recommended. Andrew Cobble at Merrick Books has been running Kickstarter campaigns for several years and understands the ins and outs of book campaign fulfillment.

Bookmobile – one-stop shop. Bookmobile can offset-print your books and also help with fulfillment to individual backers.

Vervante

Quartermaster Logistics

Efulfillment Service

FURTHER RESOURCES

- Classes And Videos
- Recommended Reading
- Kickstarter for Authors Facebook Groups
- Make Pretty Graphics
- Format Pretty Books
- Start your Newsletter
- Get Expert Help
- What Did I Miss?
- Updates to *Kickstarter for Authors*

CLASSES AND VIDEOS

Dean Wesley Smith offers a free set of prerecorded video classes on Teachable. He goes over a lot of the basics of running your first Kickstarter.

All the Ins and Outs of a Fiction Kickstarter | WMG Publishing (teachable.com)

(wmg-publishing-workshops-and-
lectures.teachable.com/p/kickstarter)

There are some great videos from 20Books Vegas that are packed with information.

20Books Vegas 2021 Day 3 -Leonelle & Nohelty - Kickstarter as a First Payment in Your Revenue Stream - YouTube (2021)

20Books Vegas 2022 Day 3 - Kickstarter Basic - YouTube (2022)

I'm sure the ones from 2023 will be up soon. Look for the great Kickstarter panel with Oriana Leckert, Joanna Penn, Russell Nohelty, and Anthea Sharp, moderated by Paddy Finn.

RECOMMENDED READING

In addition to the Kickstarter resources listed above, and this book, there are a couple more excellent books on how to crowdfund as an author. Check out the following:

Get Your Book Selling on Kickstarter by Russell Nohelty and Monica Leonelle

Crowdfunding Your Fiction by Loren Coleman

KICKSTARTER FOR AUTHORS FACEBOOK GROUPS

Come join us in the mighty and supportive groups on Facebook!

Kickstarter for Authors:

Kickstarter for Authors | Facebook

(facebook.com/ groups/429764288910415

(Experienced) Kickstarter for Authors Cross-Promo*:

(Experienced) Kickstarter for Authors Cross-Promotion | Facebook

(facebook.com/groups/408680631087020)

*Requires a link to your Kickstarter campaign to join.

MAKE PRETTY GRAPHICS

Kickstarter is a highly visual platform. As such, you need to put a lot of nice visuals in your campaign. Here are some of the programs and resources authors use to create those good-looking graphics.

- Canva
- Bookbrush
- Photoshop
- GIMP
- Affinity
- Stock photo sites like DepositPhotos

To create 3D book images, there are templates available in some of the above programs. You could also check out the following sites:

The 3D Book Cover Creator You'll Love to Use (diybookcovers.com) (my go-to)

https://smartmockups.com/

If you have zero graphic design skills, ask your cover designer or friends to help you create some strong visuals for your Kickstarter campaign. They truly are essential.

FORMAT PRETTY BOOKS

There are two great formatting programs available to authors. With them, you can create gorgeous print and eBooks with illustrations, full-page image spreads, custom chapter headers, dropcap letters at the start of chapters, etc.

If you are on a Mac, get Vellum.

If you are on a PC, get Atticus.

START YOUR NEWSLETTER

If you already have a newsletter, start a segment or second newsletter specifically for your Kickstarter backers. Invite them to join your mailing list when you send out your rewards survey, and in the occasional backer update.

If you are at sea and don't know where to start, I highly recommend you grab a copy of *Newsletter Ninja* by Tammi Labrecque. Every author should have a mailing list. It's an essential part of running your own publishing business.

GET EXPERT HELP WITH KICKSTARTER

If you're interested in a bit more help than this book provides, you can hire me for a consult! I've been consulting for authors for several years, and have a number of testimonials from clients I'd be delighted to share with you. In addition to advice on indie publishing, I offer Kickstarter consultation.

You can book an hour-long session with me, or sign up for a Kickstarter Campaign Prelaunch Flight Check if you just want eyes on your campaign to catch anything before you launch. Find out more here:

Consulting – Fiddlehead Press

(fiddleheadpress.com/collections/consulting)

WHAT DID I MISS?

In writing this book, I've tried to be as comprehensive as possible regarding how authors can best use Kickstarter. However, I'm sure I've missed a few things. If I didn't cover something you were looking for, please reach out to me! If I *did* cover something but it was just too confusing, please let me know that, too. Email me at anthea@antheasharp.com

I'd love to hear your stories about using Kickstarter. And come join the Facebook groups. See you there!

UPDATES TO *KICKSTARTER FOR AUTHORS*

NOTE: If you're reading this book in mid-2024 or later, please check the following link, where I will post twice-yearly updates regarding what has changed on Kickstarter since this book was published. These will be posted in June and December, 2024. (Meanwhile, check out the link for an extra goody...)

https://dl.bookfunnel.com/4or16k21gl

COMMON MISTAKES

- Not having a prelaunch.
- Setting your funding goal way too high.
- Making a confusing campaign with unclear reward tiers.
- Not having the book done.
- Not having cover art.
- Going overboard with swag.
- Messing up shipping.
- Not calculating an extra 10% on EVERYTHING.
- Linking your sample chapters to a required newsletter sign-up page.
- Not backing other campaigns.
- Being unprepared for wild success (it happens).

While this isn't a comprehensive list by any means, it might help you steer clear of a couple pitfalls as you prepare to set up and launch your Kickstarter campaign. Good luck!

GLOSSARY

Add-ons: Extra rewards in your campaign that backers can add once they have made a pledge.

Backer Swap: Trading campaign mentions with other creators in each of your backer updates.

Backer: Someone who has pledged to your campaign.

Backlist: Your previously published books

Book Box: A box containing a book, swag, and other themed goodies, often packaged appealingly.

Campaign: Your project.

Cancelled Pledge: Backers are free to cancel or change their pledges at any time until your campaign ends. Be prepared for this fact.

Creator: The person creating the project.

Dead Zone: The period of time when your campaign slows to almost a standstill. Usually in the middle period of your project's duration.

Drop Ship: When the printer ships the product directly from their facility to the backer. Campaign fulfillment companies will also sort and ship rewards to backers, for a fee.

Dropped Backer: If a backer's errored pledge isn't resolved seven days after your project ends, Kickstarter drops them from your campaign.

Early-bird Rewards: Items offered at the beginning of the campaign, either at a discount or with an added bonus, to encourage backers to support your campaign right away.

Errored Pledge: If a backer's credit card details don't go through, their pledge shows with a red exclamation mark on your dashboard. Kickstarter reminds them every forty-eight hours to fix their payment method. If their pledge isn't resolved after a few days, it's a good idea for the creator to reach out, too.

Flash Rewards: Limited-time rewards rolled out to tempt folks into backing your campaign, and to motivate current backers to help spread the word.

Followers: People who have clicked the "Notify me on launch" or, once live, the "Remind me" button on your campaign page who are interested, but not yet committed to backing.

Frontlist: Your newest book.

Fulfillment: Sending the products and promised rewards out (digital and physical) to backers once your campaign ends.

Funded: Your campaign reached the goal you set!

Kickstart: The act of Kickstarting your project.

Offset Printer: A printer doing a high-volume print run of books. Generally, the higher the volume, the less each book will cost to print.

Pledge Manager: Third-party businesses who can help with some aspects of your campaign. These include BackerKit, PledgeBox and PledgeManager, among others.

Pledge: The backer's promise to give a monetary amount, usually in return for certain rewards.

Prelaunch: The period of time where your campaign is approved and you have a basic page up on Kickstarter, but before your project is live. People can see your banner, title, and subtitle, and can click "Notify me on launch" so that they are alerted when your campaign launches.

Preview: The ability to let people see "behind the scenes" as you build out your campaign.

Print on Demand (POD): A process where single copies of a book can be printed. There is no minimum, but the costs stay the same regardless of number of books printed (although some POD printers will give a small discount on bulk orders).

Print Run: Multiple copies of a book printed, with a minimum order. Some printers require at least fifty books others need a minimum order of three hundred.

Project We Love: A designation given to certain campaigns that offer something special, appealing, or unique, hand-selected by Kickstarter staff. Chosen campaigns are spotlighted in different areas of the Kickstarter platform.

Project: Your campaign.

Return on investment (ROI): Your cost-to-profit margin. Some folks don't worry about running on thinner margins, as there are other, intangible, benefits to running a Kickstarter. It's not all about the money. But don't forget, your time is invested too, and that's something worth valuing as well.

Reward Tiers: The different levels backers can pledge for—like a $5 eBook, or a $50 autographed hardback with bookmark and character art prints included.

Rewards: The items you're offering to backers.

Story: The page where you explain your project to prospective backers.

Stretch Goals: An upgrade to your project, usually special-edition-related, like foiled dustjackets, sprayed edges, etc. Goals are usually unlocked when a campaign reaches certain financial milestones.

Stretch Rewards: Bonus rewards for all backers unlocked once your campaign reaches certain milestones (usually financial, but also could be a certain number of backers).

Swag: Extra goodies provided along with books. They are usually book-related items like bookmarks, character cards, prints of the cover art, stickers, etc.

Tuckerization: Naming a character, place, or item after someone, or allowing them to choose the name.

Updates: Communications sent to backers from the creator, recommended when campaign milestones are reached, or every few days, to keep your supporters in the loop and engaged with the process.

MY CAMPAIGN BREAKDOWNS & TAKEAWAYS

CAMPAIGN 1:

Title: Into the Darkwood

Into the Darkwood: Special Hardback Omnibus by Fiddlehead Press — Kickstarter

Funding amount: $7,145

Number of backers: 133

Title: Into the Darkwood

Genre: Fantasy – Trilogy omnibus

New material? No. Backlist trilogy that was in eBook and individual paperbacks

Format: Hardcover

Special Edition? No—just beautiful interior formatting with custom chapter headers

Printer: Ingram POD

International shipping? No

Signed? No—everything was drop-shipped

Swag: None

Included Kickstarter backer names in book? No

New material? No. Backlist trilogy that was in eBook and individual paperbacks

Date: March 2022

Campaign length: 21 days

Prelaunch: none

Funding goal: $500

My first campaign, in March 2022, was for a hardcover edition of an existing eBook omnibus in the fantasy romance genre. I printed it POD with Ingram, drop-shipped to backers without autographing it, and didn't make it available internationally.

The thing that helped this campaign really succeed was offering a connected backlist hardcover series. That was my most expensive tier, and my most backed one, much to my surprise and delight. Total amount funded for *Into the Darkwood* was $7,145 from 133 backers, 68% of whom came from the Kickstarter platform, according to their metrics.

Things that made this book stand out, despite not being a special edition:

- A different design on the hardcover case, separate from the dustjacket
- Illustrated chapter headers
- Full-page image spreads between the three included books
- 700+ pages of epic romantic fantasy

TAKEAWAY

While a prelaunch period of at least two weeks is recommended (to gather followers who will be notified when you hit the launch button and go live), a campaign without a prelaunch can be successful. However, that was well over a year ago, and it's definitely harder now to gain traction and visibility without one.

Kickstarter backers like fantasy books in hardcover, and are willing to scoop up related series if they like the premise and look of your campaign.

Backlist can help scale up your campaign into a higher funding level.

You don't have to do it all for your first campaign. I didn't offer international shipping (except to one backer who reached out and we figured out the cost, and they upped their pledge by that amount). I didn't offer signed books, instead simply drop-shipping Print on Demand books from Ingram.

Did I leave money on the table by not opening up to international backers? Almost certainly—but I wasn't quite sure how this Kickstarter thing would work out, and was a bit cautious to start. I'm still delighted with how this campaign went, and it was a great first experience on the platform.

CAMPAIGN 2:

Title: The Perfect Perfume and Other Tales

The Perfect Perfume & Other Tales - A Steampunk Collection by Fiddlehead Press — Kickstarter

Funding amount: $5,623

Number of backers: 165

Genre: Steampunk – Short story collection

Format: Paperback

Special Edition? No—but each story featured an illustration

Printer: Ingram POD

International Shipping? No

Signed? I had a more expensive tier for a signed copy. Some backers took me up on it; others were confused why it wasn't included

Included Kickstarter backer names in book? Yes

Swag: Printable coloring pages

New material? One new story, but mostly backlist

Date: May 2022

Campaign length: 17 days

Prelaunch: 10 days, 24 followers at launch

Funding goal: $500

Let's pause a minute here and compare these two campaigns. The funding level dropped from campaign one to campaign two, but the backers increased. This is important to note, and brings up a critical thing to consider when setting up your projects.

If your general average pledge is on the lower side, your campaign fund will be smaller.

The corollary being: if you can create more expensive tiers to appeal to backers, you will likely hit higher funding.

I know, it's obvious when you stop to consider it, but I sometimes see people thinking they can have a bunch of low-cost tiers and then magically hit five-figure (or higher!) funding. It doesn't work that way, unless you get a whole lot of backers onboard. This is why digital-only campaigns almost always have a much smaller fund, since in general eBook editions are priced much lower than physical books—that, plus Kickstarter backers generally prefer physical books. And in fantasy, hardcovers. (However, the ROI on digital is much higher, since there's not an associated cost to produce each copy the way there is with print editions.)

CAMPAIGN ONE.

My average pledge per backer was $54. Part of that was because I had hardcovers of the next trilogy available in a higher tier that included the omnibus, for $110.

CAMPAIGN TWO

My average pledge per backer dropped to $34. Why? Because the paperback was less expensive, and I don't have a large Steampunk backlist. My most-backed tier was a $9 eBook bundle that included my one Steampunk novel along with the short story collection. Still, it was a strong campaign, and I got thirty-two more backers than my first campaign.

For this second campaign, I felt more secure about adding something like signed books, and including the backer's names in both the eBook and paperback editions. I still didn't do international shipping (and probably lost some backers due to that).

Could I have put this into hardcover? Yes, but all my other story collections are just in paperback, and wanted to keep consistency. I could definitely see doing some hardcover collections down the line, though.

TAKEAWAY

An upward build from campaign to campaign on Kickstarter doesn't always mean more money. Sometimes it means you reached more backers, which in many ways can be even more valuable if you intend to make Kickstarter part of your long-term career.

Less backlist meant I didn't have a lot to beef up the higher tiers of this campaign, though I did add my one related novel, and all my story collections. A number of folks pledged for the full story collections, and some even added on the fantasy books from my first campaign.

Funding over $5.5k to put a backlist short story collection into print felt amazing.

CAMPAIGN 3:

Title: AI Dreaming: Palindromes

AI DREAMING: Palindromes - Illustrated with Midjourney AI by Fiddlehead Press — Kickstarter

Funding amount: $2,544

Number of backers: 74

Genre: Quirky palindrome art book

Format: eBook, paperback, & hardcover

Special Edition? No—but was full color illustrations printed on high-quality paper

Printer: Lulu POD

International Shipping? Yes

Signed? No

Included Kickstarter backer names in book? No

Swag: Postcard of the cover art included with all pledges. Digital wallpapers, bonus images, and art card add-ons

New material? Yes

Date: September 2022

Campaign length: 21 days

Prelaunch: 2 weeks, 26 followers at launch

Funding goal: $500

This was a completely oddball project, not fiction at all. I learned a ton about printing quality art books, and about how inexpensive Lulu is for international drop-shipping (but not, alas, for the printing itself). International supporters counted for a decent percentage of pledges on this campaign, and learning how to drop-ship from a POD printer gave me the confidence to add international shipping to all my subsequent campaigns.

Interestingly, though this was something entirely different from my first two campaigns, I had several repeat backers hop on board. Many Kickstarter backers are small-scale angel investors, happy to support a creator they like, regardless of what you're making. This was a delightful thing to learn.

I'm happy with how this campaign went. It was a super-small niche, but still funded respectably, with no backlist to offer, and just a few add-ons like art cards.

TAKEAWAY

Some supporters will support *you*, the creator, regardless of what you make. It's their chance to be patrons of the arts, and help individual artists via the Kickstarter platform. I find that to be one of the wonderful things about using Kickstarter.

I eased into both international shipping and physical swag with this campaign, and gained the confidence to continue to offer both those things.

CAMPAIGN 4:

Title: Feyland books 1-3

The FEYLAND Trilogy 10th Anniversary Special Hardcovers by Fiddlehead Press — Kickstarter

Funding amount: $18,600

Number of backers: 261

Genre: Fantasy (with gaming elements)

Format: Hardcover

Special Edition? Anniversary hardcover editions, signed and numbered, bonus illustrations, custom headers, special under-case designs. BUT no foiling, edges, etc.

Printer: Ingram POD

International Shipping? Yes

Signed? Yes

Included Kickstarter backer names in book? No

Swag: Cover art postcards, character cards

New material? Unlocked stretch reward of a brand-new story, but the books were backlist

Date: October 2022

Campaign length: 27 days

Prelaunch: @3 months, 118 followers at launch

Funding goal: $1000

The majority of my supporters backed the hardcover editions of the trilogy, with the eBook editions coming in second. My average pledge was up to $74 this time around—again, because many folks pledged for the $130 hardcover tier (U.S. shipping included, international shipping fairly reasonable).

Backlist played some part, but I knew I wanted to do a second campaign for the next three books in the series, so I didn't really push those books. A lot of folks showed up for this (261 backers!), and I think it's because it's my *USA Today* bestselling series, never before in hardcover. The combination of a lot of backers plus a bigger average pledge = a higher-funding campaign.

That said, there was an excruciating period where I was stuck in the $14k range for days and days and days (eight, to be exact). A flash goal finally got things moving again—I should have tried that a lot earlier.

Because I was offering all copies signed (a first for me), I had to figure out how to do that for international backers. I used Ingram Spark's personalization feature to digitally sign and personalize books to backers. Two of them were sent to the wrong backers, but Ingram rectified their mistake. In the future, I'll probably send signed book plates, or print in a digital signature without personalization for all Kickstarter editions. Some authors have had very poor results using the personalization feature, where Ingram sent the books out randomly and many backers didn't get the copy that was supposed to be personalized for them, resulting in a huge headache all the way around.

TAKEAWAY

This campaign was a full four weeks, but one of those weeks was absolutely stagnant in terms of pledges. Yes, I got new backers, but I also saw a number of cancellations, and so the funding amount went up a little, then down a little, then up a little. In the future, I'd trim back to three weeks, to try to avoid so much of the saggy middle.

This was my first campaign where I set a funding goal of $1000, and hit it pretty quickly out of the gate. I felt good about bumping up into four-figure goal territory, and I do advise that once you've run a few campaigns, think about adjusting that goal upward. Even though I advocate that it's a floor, not a ceiling, having a goal of $1k or more that you hit quickly can definitely show that you have confidence in your campaign. Just make sure it's not misplaced. Funding velocity is an important metric within Kickstarter.

If you want to break into the five figures with a campaign, offer spendier-yet-appealing tiers (a hardback trilogy, in this case) and, ideally, bring a lot of backers to the table.

WHAT I'D DO DIFFERENTLY:

Shorter campaign length. I think I'll roll back to twenty-one days, in hopes of avoiding that saggy middle.

Fewer tiers. I mean, honestly, seventeen? That's a little nuts.

Put my live reading stretch reward way earlier so that I could use the video to pump up interest for the Kickstarter.

Not get COVID and be travelling while trying to fulfill signed book rewards. That was brutal.

WHAT WORKED:

Launching with over one hundred followers gave a great initial boost!

I baked-in the under-jacket artwork as a stretch reward. That was the only one I announced a dollar figure goal for in advance, because I knew we'd hit it and I wanted folks to get excited.

Character cards were fun, and a hit.

This was the first time I did early-bird rewards (not time-limited but amount-limited), and I think people liked the extra goody. (It was a bonus exclusive postcard.)

Lots of stretches and add-ons like bonus art and character cards, and a new story. I tried to include things that were of interest to all tiers and backer levels.

CAMPAIGN 5:

Title: Faerie Hearts: A Romantic Fantasy Collection

Faerie Hearts: A Romantic Fantasy Collection by Fiddlehead Press — Kickstarter

Funding amount: $7,701

Number of backers: 228

Genre: Romantic fantasy

Format: Paperback

Special Edition? Special duplex covers, black-and-white illustrations

Printer: Ingram POD

International Shipping? Yes

Signed? No—but physical backers got a signed bookplate mailed to them

Included Kickstarter backer names in book? Yes

Swag: Bookmark included with every tier, printable coloring pages, digital wallpapers

New material? Yes! My first frontlist project

Date: February 2023

Campaign length: 17 days

Prelaunch: 2 months, 93 followers at launch

Funding goal: $1000

Interestingly, just like my other short story collection, this one also had a $34 average pledge, and ran for the same number of days (seventeen). However, this time around I had sixty-three more backers. There could be several reasons for this, including a general build of supporters on the platform over the previous four campaigns, a longer prelaunch period (I launched with sixty-nine more followers this time), and the fact it was a frontlist release, so would appeal to my existing readers as well as new-to-me backers. I also included international shipping this time around, and had a tiny bit of swag included (a bookmark).

TAKEAWAY

I think Kickstarter backers like to see their names in print as supporters. Some campaigns include this at only the top tiers. I included them for backers at a certain dollar amount and above (the $5 level). I suspect this might encourage folks to step up to the print editions. However, the logistics of adding over two hundred and fifty names into the thank-yous can be a little daunting.

This story collection was more firmly in the fantasy genre, which probably also made a difference. I leaned on the romantic elements, as I launched this campaign right around Valentine's Day. Working to theme on the platform can be a good way to make your campaign more appealing, as well.

This was my first frontlist book launch on Kickstarter, and I'm really pleased with how it went. Backers got their rewards several months before retailer release. I didn't see any cannibalization of sales from the Kickstarter, plus I got to launch this book completely in the black, which definitely reduces release-day anxiety on the retailers.

Currently, I plan to launch my new books on Kickstarter first, then my online store, then on retailers. This is the way.

CAMPAIGN 6:

Title: Feyland books 4-6

Feyland 10th Anniversary Hardcovers - The Feyguard! by Fiddlehead Press — Kickstarter

Funding amount: $15,442

Number of backers: 172

Genre: Fantasy (with gaming elements)

Format: Hardcovers

Special Edition? Second half of the Anniversary editions, signed and numbered, bonus illustrations, custom headers, special under-case designs. BUT no foiling, edges, etc.

Printer: Ingram POD

International Shipping? Yes

Signed? Yes

Included Kickstarter backer names in book? No

Swag: Cover art postcards, character cards, digital art

New material? No

Date: May 2023

Campaign length: 21 days

Prelaunch: 2+ months, 220 followers at launch

Funding goal: $3000

Based on the first Feyland campaign, I set funding goal for this one at three thousand dollars. In retrospect, this may have slowed my initial velocity a little. This campaign funded lower than the first, but the average pledge was up at $90—a record for me so far!

This was because I had a number of takers for the entire series, Books 1-6, in hardcover. I also had most of my backers from the first campaign return for this next set of books.

However, I'd already tapped out the digital backers, for the most part. In the first Feyland campaign, over sixty percent of my backers supported the digital tiers, including the full omnibus (which I offered in the first campaign as well as the second). For this campaign, the number of backers in digital tiers dropped to just over fifty percent. That ten percent difference, with fewer backers, is part of why I had a lower campaign fund (but also why my average pledge was higher).

During the time this campaign was running, there were also dreary economic forecasts coming out, and I hit the start of summer vacation for many schools (May into June), which I think also had an impact. As with everything, there can be factors beyond our control, and we have to roll with it. Not that I'm complaining—I raised over $15k! But I must admit I had higher hopes based on the first campaign, which raised $18,600.

TAKEAWAY

There's a delicate balance between offering new things to your core fans, appealing to former backers, and bringing new supporters in. I didn't strike that as well as I could have in this campaign, and it was a good reminder to consider all the bases going forward.

Also, the interplay between digital and physical tiers, especially with a completed series, is an interesting one to try to figure out. Do you hold back the full series in digital if you're just doing half the series in your first campaign? On one hand, you're leaving potential money on the table by not offering everything, but on the other, you might be taking a big bite out of that apple that then hollows out the second campaign a bit. I don't think there's a right answer, but it's interesting to ponder.

The final thing I saw on this particular campaign was a solid bump to my Feyland series on all retailers. The fact of the Kickstarter campaign, and my many posts about it and my series, raised the overall visibility and resulted in more book sales off-platform. So that was a nice added bonus.

CAMPAIGN 7:

Title: Kickstarter for Authors

Kickstarter for Authors: Helping Writers Fund and Flourish by Fiddlehead Press — Kickstarter

Funding goal: $1000

Final funding amount: $11,251

Number of backers: 497

Genre: Nonfiction (this book!)

Format: eBook, paperback, hardcover

Special Edition? No

Printer: Ingram POD

International Shipping? Yes

Signed? No

Included Kickstarter backer names in book? No

Swag: Printable tips sheet and launch checklist, Zoom AMA

New material? Yes

Date: August 2023

Campaign length: 21 days

Prelaunch: 1 month, 249 followers at launch

Conversion from followers to backers: 49%

Errored pledges: 6 ($250 total) but one backer paid via PayPal, so only 5 got away

This campaign (to help create the very book you're reading right now) was obviously a departure from my fantasy-adjacent fiction titles! The funding raise is lower than my big hardcover campaigns (I did offer a hardcover edition, but most folks prefer paperback or eBook for their nonfiction reads).

This campaign is also a perfect illustration of how the *average pledge amount + number of backers = potential funding* equation works. The campaign before this one I had fewer than two hundred backers, but my average pledge was $90, so that one funded over $15k. This one, I had almost five hundred backers (so awesome!) but the average pledge was way lower. That's how the math works. If you don't get a lot of people pledging to higher-priced tiers, then your funding will be lower, unless you make up for it in sheer numbers.

Unlike other nonfiction authors, I don't have classes or workshops or paywalled communities set up to monetize this side of my writing. And I don't really want to! I make my living as a fiction writer, and don't have the time or energy to completely retool as an instructor (though I love teaching, almost as much as writing and publishing).

Actually, I do offer paid consults on a low-key basis. I've been an indie author since 2011 (traditionally published before that) and a full-time author for the past decade. I've seen some stuff, let's just say, and I really DO love helping other authors—which is why I started the Kickstarter for Authors group on Facebook (come join us!), and why I wrote this book. I'm not in nonfiction to make bank. I just want to reach folks who could benefit from this information.

For me, success on this campaign was having the support of almost five hundred backers. Thank you.

That said, I did add a few extras to try to get the average pledge level up—and even created something new for my casual business side of things: the Campaign Prelaunch Flight Check. This is a final check through your campaign to identify any potential issues, give feedback, and let you know what looks great as well as what might need further tweaking. (You can sign up for one of these, or a full consult, at: Consulting – Fiddlehead Press)

The vast majority of supporters on this campaign jumped in at the $10 eBook level. Having 68% of backers go for the digital tiers means fulfillment is simpler, and the profit margin is higher than on the tiers where I'm paying to print and ship a lot of books. This campaign brought in as much profit as my last one, even though it funded four thousand dollars lower. Just something to think about.

But as I said, profit wasn't my main goal here. Training my competition was! (According to my husband, haha.)

I honestly see having more authors on Kickstarter not as competition, but as a way to build a vibrant, successful book ecosystem. The more that getting a book via a Kickstarter campaign becomes "normal," the more readers will head over to the platform. And that benefits everyone.

Readers get something awesome, usually with extra goodies.

Authors aren't giving up 35%-75% percent of the sales to a faceless retailer.

Backers get to be small-scale angel investors and patrons of the arts.

Authors get to connect on a personal basis with the people who are supporting our careers.

Everybody wins! (Except the big corporate retailers...)

TAKEAWAY

I probably won't do a nonfiction campaign again (though I never say never!). I love setting up and running campaigns for my fiction, and I love writing those books. Kickstarter for Authors has been a labor of love. I'm delighted it's out there in the world (partly because now I can go back to my novels, lol).

CAMPAIGN 8:

Title: The Duke's Christmas

The Duke's Christmas: Dainty Paperback Edition by Fiddlehead Press — Kickstarter

Funding goal: $500

Final funding amount: $1,465

Number of backers: 70

Average pledge per backer: $21

Genre: Historical romance

Format: Mass-market-size paperback

Special Edition? No

Printer: Ingram POD

International Shipping? Yes

Signed? Yes

Included Kickstarter backer names in book? Yes

Swag: Gingerbread recipe, bonus short story

New material? No

Date: September 2023

Campaign length: 17 days

Prelaunch: 2 weeks, 41 followers at launch

Conversion from followers to backers: 32%

Errored pledges: 0

This was set up to be a low-stress campaign. It originally had only three titles: a short story (going out to all backers), the main title (*The Duke's Christmas*), and another holiday book. I offered eBook and paperback only. When I was first putting together this campaign, I put all my romance backlist in (four more print books, plus a half dozen more eBooks and collections), but then decided I'd rather have a smaller funding raise and less stress in terms of trying to get books fulfilled in time for the holidays. As is, I had pledges for thirty-seven physical copies, but some of those will be drop-shipped, so I'll end up signing and shipping out about 33 books. That's about 10% of my last big Feyland campaign, which will feel so easy in comparison.

Midway through the campaign, I decided to add a new tier (digital only) featuring two more holiday-themed titles. I put those in the add-ons too, along with a collection of sweet short stories. That helped bump the campaign up and got me out of a flatline period.

I offered three stretch rewards, and tried to set them at points that would help keep things moving. I also made sure they'd all be unlocked by forty-eight hours before the campaign ended. Those stretches were all digital—backer names in a Thank You section of the book, a traditional gingerbread recipe, and a bonus short holiday story added to the main book (which I was pretty much planning to add all along).

My profit margin on this one will come out to about 65%— maybe a touch more. I'll know after the shipping is done.

TAKEAWAY

This campaign illustrates the point that *genre matters*. So much. Of my seventy backers, about thirty were return backers who had pledged to my campaigns before. Without them, I would have had closer to forty backers. Romance without any paranormal or fantasy elements does not yet have super-strong support on Kickstarter. It's not of *no* interest, luckily, and I'm pleased with how this campaign went. I'll do another holiday historical romance campaign next year and see what happens then. But I'm not in any rush to create hardcover editions of my backlist romance novels.

Final thoughts

I hope you enjoyed reading these campaign breakdowns and found them useful! People post similar breakdowns in the Kickstarter for Authors group pretty much every week. Come join us if you're not already a member. Kickstarter for Authors | Facebook

COMPREHENSIVE CAMPAIGN CHECKLIST

COMPREHENSIVE CAMPAIGN CHECKLIST

Check off these steps to make sure you didn't miss anything!

NAVIGATING KICKSTARTER

PROJECT SETUP

PRELAUNCH

LAUNCH

CAMPAIGN IS LIVE

FINAL FEW DAYS & END

POST-CAMPAIGN

FULFILLMENT

WHAT IF YOU DON'T FUND

NAVIGATING KICKSTARTER

☐ **Make a Kickstarter account** and start exploring the platform. https://www.kickstarter.com/

☐ Discover the **Discover search function** (on the upper left, which is *not* the regular search on the upper right). Check out books in Publishing > Fiction > Just Launched. The search defaults to Projects We Love. Go through the search results, then uncheck the Projects We Love selection and explore everything that's currently running. Look at banners, titles, funding goals. Notice what's struggling as well as what's succeeding.

☐ **Back projects** you like the look of! Best practice is to support several campaigns before launching your own. This will give you important info about how backer updates work, as well as showing that you're part of the Kickstarter community before you launch your own project.

☐ **Do your research.** Read books on how to run Kickstarter campaigns, hunt up free videos and classes, join the Kickstarter for Authors group on Facebook.

☐ Expect the entire process of running a Kickstarter from start to finish to take a *minimum* of three months, and probably more like four-plus. Research, setting up your campaign, prelaunch period, live, and post-campaign fulfillment **all will take longer than you think!**

PROJECT SETUP

☐ **Decide what your project will be** and study the heck out of similar, successful campaigns that have run on Kickstarter.

☐ Figure out your **budget**. There are some good videos and articles out there about how to do this—check out Kickstarter's creator resources. Use the printing and shipping calculators at Ingram or the other POD platforms to see how much your book will cost. (Sometimes you'll have to reach out for a direct quote, or go through as if you're setting up the book to be printed.)

☐ Figure out the **shipping**. This can be a somewhat involved process. *Kickstarter for Authors* goes into it in lots of detail. Decide whether to drop-ship or get the books shipped to you for you to sign, package and ship. Estimate accordingly. You may want to look into Pirate Ship or similar shipping consolidators.

☐ Click "**Start a Project**" from the upper-left of any Kickstarter page. Exciting!

THE BASICS

☐ Start inputting your project's basic information. Create a clear, descriptive **title** and a keyword-rich **subtitle**. The title should clearly describe what you're offering. Not just "Winterset" but "Winterset: Epic Fantasy Hardcover Edition." Think of the subtitle as your seven keyword boxes on a certain retailer. This and the title are where Kickstarter indexes its search terms. Use all the characters, if you can, and use them wisely.

☐ Choose your **category**. Publishing, then whatever is the best fit.

☐ Choose a **secondary category**. This is an optional field and not currently used for search results or project placement by Kickstarter. Maybe someday.

☐ Set a **location**. This could be your hometown or nearby big city. Up to you. If your project is deeply rooted in a specific locale, consider going with that.

☐ Create an **uncluttered banner**. This is important because potential backers will see your banner at one-sixth size when browsing Kickstarter (or at even smaller sizes on their mobile device). Avoid text, for the most part. Entice prospective backers with something visually rich. I generally recommend you put a 3D book mockup on your banner—hardcover if you're offering that.

☐ **Video!** Keep it short and sweet—no more than two minutes. Ninety seconds is even better. Be real; be enthusiastic about your project. A polished trailer isn't necessary. Don't rely only on the video to convey important information. Make sure to also include it in the written project story. Half your backers probably won't watch your video. (Posting a video is optional, but highly recommended.)

☐ Set your **funding goal**. The common wisdom is $500 for first-time book campaigns (unless your project won't get made without a certain amount raised, a special edition, for example). Remember, the funding goal is a floor, not a ceiling. A quick funding goal has its advantages.

☐ Target **launch date**. Be aware that this isn't like a preorder. Kickstarter *does not* auto-launch your project for you. It's an optional field, but helpful for planning your prelaunch schedule.

☐ Set your **campaign duration.** I recommend between seventeen and twenty-one days, especially for a first-time project. You have two options here. If you want the campaign to end at a specific time of day, choose the "ends on specific day and time" option. Otherwise the campaign will end at the same time of day that it launched. Either way, you will still need to manually launch your project when you're ready.

☐ When is the **best time to end?** It's a bit situational, but be aware that Kickstarter will send out a notice to people who have followed but not backed your campaign at the forty-eight- and eight-hour marks. Think about when it might be good for those folks to receive and open those notifications.

Also, Kickstarter releases funds fourteen days after your campaign ends. If you close on a Friday after five p.m. EST, you may have to wait longer than fourteen days, depending on your bank, any holidays, etc.

Yay, you finished the Basics! Time for backer REWARDS

☐ Figure out your **Reward Tiers,** with a nice range of inexpensive to high-ticket tiers. Ten tiers, max, is recommended, unless you have a compelling reason for more. Ask yourself if some of the items are better as add-ons instead. Keep things clear and easy to follow. Add item images. Make sure you fill out all the fields here—this area can get fussy with dates, in particular.

Keep in mind that Reward Tiers are not stackable. Backers can pledge to only one.

☐ Figure out your **Add-ons**. This is a good place to put backlist, extra swag, etc. Backers cannot access the add-ons until they make a pledge. There are also some tricky things about physical versus digital rewards, and what add-ons can be added to which reward tiers. I cover that in depth in *Kickstarter for Authors*.

☐ Build in extra time for fulfillment, especially for print rewards. Figure out the month you think you'll deliver, then *add another month*. Under-promise, over-deliver.

Remember, you can keep tweaking your rewards, add-ons, and items until your campaign launches. Build out the basics, get your campaign approved for prelaunch, then come back and continue to refine.

Now, to the heart of your campaign—the STORY!

☐ Create your project Story. Use an enticing hook up top and lots of art and graphics! *Think like a backer*. Don't make the campaign about what YOU want and need as an author. I don't recommend an approach like "I need money to publish, and I want an editor and a new cover." Backers don't care. What do THEY get? Maybe "Support this campaign and get a fabulous fantasy adventure with a gorgeous, newly illustrated cover!" is a better approach. Entice browsers. Tell them what's awesome and engaging and unique about your book and what they get from backing your campaign—whether it's an awesome read, or a fancy book. Or both!

☐ I recommend you lead with what your book is about. In certain genres, trope graphics or lists of tropes can be very effective. Let prospective backers know right away what they're getting. Is this their kind of read?

☐ If this is a special edition, definitely show off what you're offering. But interest readers in what's *inside* the book first, and then talk about the gorgeous packaging second.

☐ Include a link for folks to go read a sample.

☐ If this is for a previously published book, put in a couple glowing review quotes.

☐ Have a section showing off and talking about the Rewards. Have another one about the Add-ons.

☐ Finally, introduce yourself. Backers are now interested in knowing a bit about who you are as a creator.

☐ I always recommend a *Why Kickstarter* section, too. Why are you using the platform instead of just releasing on retailers?

☐ Think about whether you want to use a Stretch Reward strategy and how best to implement it.

☐ Fill out the Risks section. Shipping delays are common ones. Printing issues, paper shortages—these things happen. Make it clear if your book is finished and the artwork done. Reassure backers that you'll be transparent in your communications if delays occur.

☐ Check your campaign's appearance on your mobile device. Quite a few backers are on mobile (35% for my most recent campaign). How does that banner look? Can you read your text? Are the graphics too tiny to see?

☐ Make sure you're not using language that will prevent campaign approval. Kickstarter isn't a retailer, so don't use words like "preorder" or "sale" or "presale" in your text. You can explain your campaign off-platform using these terms, but not on Kickstarter itself.

☐ Break up big blocks of text with smaller banner graphics or evocative artwork. Use the book cover, character art, graphics that match the mood of your story and genre. While you're building your campaign, you can put placeholders like [artwork here] and fill in later with the good stuff. But please, avoid wall-of-text syndrome.

☐ I do not recommend a pie-chart financial breakdown, unless you're justifying a very high funding goal (or building a rocket to Mars).

Now you're at the PEOPLE section...

☐ Give yourself a good, personable bio.

☐ **Vanity URL**—This will be used by Kickstarter to create a URL for all your projects on Kickstarter. Use your **pen name or press name** here. If you use your project name you will be stuck with it as your identifier on all your Kickstarter projects forevermore.

☐ A quick note about privacy and pen names on Kickstarter. You can create a campaign for any name, but be aware that Kickstarter *shows your legal name* on your profile. They pull from your tax and banking info. In order to protect your privacy as an author, you'll need to reach out to pwlsupport@kickstarter.com and ask them to fix that once your campaign has been approved. You will need to do this each time for every campaign you create.

☐ Fill in the other fields as appropriate.

Now the fun part... PAYMENT INFO!

☐ Go through the steps one at a time. If you filled out the previous step and you can't move forward, try **refreshing** the page.

☐ The final payment source is for refunds or chargebacks (uncommon), but still required.

PROMOTION SECTION

☐ **Project URL**. This is autogenerated from your project title (and vanity URL). This is the address where your project lives on the web.

☐ **Prelaunch page**. Once Kickstarter approves your project, you must come back here and click the Activate button! And then confirm again from the prelaunch page that's generated. A prelaunch page allows people to follow your campaign before it goes live. You can also see your follower count here.

☐ **Custom referral tags** are your friends! You can create up to five hundred (!!) of them. Use one for your newsletter, one for each social media platform, one for your mom to share with friends, etc. When your campaign goes live, you'll be able to see on your dashboard what links backers followed to support your campaign.

☐ **Analytics**. Set up any of the ones you've got. Data is good, but not mandatory.

☐ Once you've got the basics sketched out, put your campaign in for Kickstarter approval. Your project does NOT

NEED TO BE COMPLETELY FINISHED at this point. You want to get a prelaunch page up early for backers to follow, but you can't do this until your campaign is approved by Kickstarter.

PRELAUNCH

☐ Once your project is **approved**, DO NOT CLICK THE BIG GREEN BUTTON (it will launch your campaign immediately).

☐ **Create the Prelaunch page**—*do* click the Activate button on the Promotions page. That will create the prelaunch page. Don't worry, this page will only show your title, subtitle, and banner. Nobody can see your full campaign yet unless you share the preview link.

☐ Gather **followers**. Best practice is to have a prelaunch for two weeks, minimum, to gather up folks who will be notified when your campaign goes live. I'm currently recommending you try to collect a bare minimum of twenty-five backers before launch. Fifty is even better.

☐ Get feedback on your campaign using the **preview share.** (Look for the "enable sharing" link on the upper left of your menu page.)

☐ Post your **campaign video** to social media.

☐ **Warm up your readers** and fans to Kickstarter. Explain what the platform is (and is *not*—plenty of people think it's like GoFundMe). Share projects you've backed and encourage your readers to do the same.

LAUNCH

☐ What are the **best times** to launch? I recommend in the morning when most of the U.S. is awake. Weekdays are preferable, and a lot of creators tend to launch on Tuesdays. I've seen campaigns launch successfully on every day of the week.

☐ Kickstarter doesn't auto-launch your campaign for you, despite the fact that you may have put in a target date when you set up your project. It will, however, auto-end to the date or duration you set. When ready, **CLICK THE GREEN BUTTON.** Your campaign will immediately launch.

☐ If you are the kind of person who loves to do **livestreams**, launch your campaign live on the platform of your choice. Get your fans involved in that initial energy rush.

☐ **You did it!** Your campaign is live. Now the fun begins. Okay, and the stress.

☐ You will immediately get lots of **spam** from people who want your $ in return for their help promoting your campaign. I guarantee they *cannot* help you. Really—they can't. Resist the urge to set your dollars on fire. Report as spam to Kickstarter, and delete/ignore. If they are contacting you off-platform, still tell the folks at Kickstarter (support@kickstarter.com).

☐ Definitely **shout from the rooftops** that your campaign is live!

☐ Watch your **funding progress**, or go distract yourself, but try not to stress for the rest of the day.

☐ Be aware that, if you launched with a bang, the funding velocity for the first couple days will **not sustain** that same upward trajectory for the rest of the campaign. Even Brandon Sanderson had slow days during his epic campaign.

CAMPAIGN IS LIVE

☐ Once you **fund** (with a little cushion to spare), make a public Update celebrating the fact. Post on your socials. Tell your fans!

☐ Announce a reasonable funding amount to unlock the first **Stretch Reward,** based on how your funding has been going. Don't set it too high—your campaign velocity WILL slow down.

☐ Continue to **tweak and refine** your campaign! You can edit everything but the funding goal, timeline, and any reward tiers that have been pledged for.

☐ Keep an eye out for any **messages/comments** you get from backers who might have questions or want you to add a new reward tier, etc. Respond promptly.

☐ You may or may not get a **Project We Love**. These are hand-selected by Kickstarter staff and usually don't show up until a few days after you've launched. Don't worry if you don't get one—your campaign will still do fine if you set it up using best practices.

☐ Consider sending a **thank-you** message when new backers pledge to your project.

☐ Know that some backers will **cancel** their pledges. This is normal. Try not to take it personally.

☐ Prepare for the **slow days**, when you might get no pledges, or even go backwards in your funding amount. Again, *this is normal*. Painful, but normal.

☐ **Cross-promote** your campaign with other Kickstarter creators on the platform. The Experienced Kickstarter for Authors Cross-promo Facebook group is a great resource for setting up backer swaps and boosts.

☐ Send an **update** every three to four days telling backers about how the campaign is going, any new tiers or added shipping locations, unlocked Stretches, extra artwork/up-grades, etc.

☐ Throughout your campaign, continue to **promote** it on your social media and to your mailing list. I personally don't hit my list too hard and mostly rely on the bulk of the promotion to happen via socials and cross-promotion on Kickstarter with other creators.

FINAL FEW DAYS & END

☐ Keep promoting. Lean on the **time-limited nature** of the platform. Emphasize that folks will miss out on the special goodies / unlocked rewards if they don't act soon.

☐ Stay excited and engaged; roll out those **final perks.**

☐ You cannot see or interact with people who are **Following** but have not pledged, but Kickstarter will send them a reminder email forty-eight hours and eight hours before your campaign ends.

☐ Before the forty-eight-hour mark, move your unlocked Stretches and / or upgrades and bonus goodies up near the **top of your campaign** to entice those followers to become backers.

☐ Hope for an **uptick** of pledges at the end (not guaranteed, but not uncommon).

☐ Watch your last five minutes **count down** on your campaign page. There's confetti!

☐ **Exhale** a huge sigh and give yourself a reward.

POST-CAMPAIGN

☐ Send a **"we did it!" update** thanking all your backers for their support. It's also a good idea to include a "what happens next" timeline so that folks know when to expect their surveys and rewards.

☐ **Edit the pledge button** on your front page to redirect people who missed your Kickstarter to a place where they can find or order your books. Google form, your direct store, prelaunch page, etc.

☐ Check for **errored pledges**. At day three, reach out to those backers encouraging them to fix their payment details. Do this via the message system on Kickstarter, and if you don't get a quick response, email them directly.

☐ Kickstarter will drop backers from your campaign if they haven't corrected their payments by day seven.

☐ About two weeks after your campaign ends, Kickstarter will send you your money. Bank holidays and weekends can delay your payment.

☐ Send out your **Backer Surveys** (these are available once your campaign finishes). Some creators wait a week, some send right away, some wait until payment or even later.

☐ Start **fulfilling** your rewards!

FULFILLMENT

☐ Use the Backer Survey **info** to send out your rewards.

☐ Kickstarter can help you keep track of what items and amounts you'll need to send out. Check out the **Fulfillment** section. (But be aware that it does NOT update to dropped pledges—math accordingly.)

☐ Keep your backers in the loop! **Update regularly** as rewards are sent—digital, print, etc.

☐ Be 100% **transparent** about any delays or issues that crop up. Backers don't mind delays as long as you are communicating about what's going on.

☐ As you send out rewards, **mark them as "fulfilled"** for each backer in the Backer Report.

☐ Once all the rewards are fulfilled to the best of your ability, make a **public update** on your project, letting everyone know that all campaign rewards are out.

☐ Now you can put your **next campaign** in for approval and start all over again!

WHAT IF YOU DON'T FUND?

☐ **You learned**, and that's worth a lot.

☐ See if you can **figure out why** your campaign didn't reach the mark, and where you could do better next time.

☐ **Try again.** Plenty of creators don't fund their first campaign. It's okay. There's no black mark or anything that goes on your account. Backers also know that frequently projects don't make it. Remember, 61% of Kickstarter campaigns don't successfully reach their funding goal.

WANT A PRINTABLE PDF OF THIS CHECKLIST?

Awesome! In return for signing up for my Kickstarter-only email list I'd be delighted to give you a printable version of this 12-page checklist.

Grab your copy here: https://dl.bookfunnel.com/dbzzz6ogjh

And don't forget I give Kickstarter consults! Find out more here: Consulting – Fiddlehead Press

ACKNOWLEDGMENTS

This book wouldn't exist without the fabulous members of the Kickstarter for Authors group on Facebook. Through answering questions and sharing the excitement of what's possible on Kickstarter, we've built a powerful network and incredible community. In particular I want to thank the steadfast and helpful moderators: Tom Carpenter, Thorn Coyle, Day Leitao, Amy Wegner Campbell, Rose Dewar, Nicolette Andrews, and Katy Rank Lev. Your hard work behind the scenes is greatly appreciated!

My husband and long-time writing partner, Lawson, brought his master's degree in Adult Education to the organization of this book. Thank you so much for bringing coherence out of the optimistic chaos of my thoughts!

Thanks also to Russell Nohelty and Monica Leonelle for being pioneers in this space. You set the firm foundation for so many authors to build upon.

A huge shoutout to Oriana, Libby, Raúl with PWL Support, and all the other folks at Kickstarter who work hard to help care for creators and backers. You guys rock.

As ever, my amazing copy editor Arran McNichol came through with flying colors, despite delays on my end. Thanks, too, to Ginger for those early first-reads of key chapters.

Kim Killion at The Killion Group turns out strong covers without fail. Thanks for the design work on this one!

OTHER WORKS

THE DARKWOOD CHRONICLES

Deep in the Darkwood, a magical doorway leads to the enchanted and dangerous land of the Dark Elves~

ELFHAME

HAWTHORNE

RAINE

HEART of the FOREST (novella)

WHITE AS FROST

BLACK AS NIGHT

RED AS FLAME

SHORT STORY COLLECTIONS

TALES OF FEYLAND & FAERIE

TALES OF MUSIC & MAGIC

THE FAERIE GIRL & OTHER TALES

THE PERFECT PERFUME & OTHER TALES

COFFEE & CHANGE

MERMAID SONG

ABOUT THE AUTHOR

Growing up, Anthea Sharp spent most of her summers raiding the library shelves and reading, especially fantasy. She now makes her home in the sunny Southern California, where she writes, plays the fiddle, and tries not to game *too* much. Visit her website at antheasharp.com, friend her on Facebook, and be the first to know about new releases and reader perks by subscribing to Anthea's new release newsletter, Sharp Tales, at www.subscribepage.com/AntheaSharp

In addition to writing *USA Today* bestselling fantasy, Anthea has helped hundreds of authors with her consultations as the owner of Indie Compass Consulting. She is also the founder of the mighty Kickstarter for Authors on Facebook.

Discover more about her books and consulting services at fiddleheadpress.com.